ACCOUNTABILITY AND CHOICE IN SCHOOLING

LAW AND POLITICAL CHANGE

Series Editors: Professor Cosmo Graham, Law School, University of Hull, and Professor Norman Lewis, Centre for Socio-Legal Studies, University of Sheffield.

Current titles:

Scott Davidson: *Human Rights*
Mike Feintuck: *Accountability and Choice in Schooling*
Norman Lewis and Patrick Birkinshaw: *When Citizens Complain*
Michael Moran and Tony Prosser (eds): *Privatization and Regulatory Change in Europe*
Michael Moran and Bruce Wood: *States, Regulation and the Medical Profession*
Mary Seneviratne: *Ombudsmen in the Public Sector*

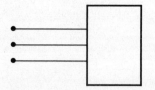

ACCOUNTABILITY AND CHOICE IN SCHOOLING

Mike Feintuck

OPEN UNIVERSITY PRESS
Buckingham • Philadelphia

Open University Press
Celtic Court
22 Ballmoor
Buckingham
MK18 1XW

and

1900 Frost Road, Suite 101
Bristol, PA 19007, USA

First Published 1994

A catalogue record of this book is available from the British Library

ISBN 0 335 15730 0 (pbk)   0 335 15731 9 (hbk)

Library of Congress Cataloging-in-Publication Data

Feintuck, Mike, 1961–
    Accountability and choice in schooling / Mike Feintuck.
      p. cm.
    Includes bibliographical references and index.
      ISBN 0–335–15731–9   ISBN 0–335–15730–0 (pbk.)
      1. Education and state — Great Britain. 2. School management and
organization — Great Britain. 3. Educational accountability — Great Britain.
4. Educational change — Great Britain. I. Title.
LC93.G7F45 1994
379.41 — dc20   93–38387
                                                                      CIP

Typeset by Colset Private Limited, Singapore
Printed in Great Britain by Biddles Ltd, Guildford and Kings Lynn

To my parents

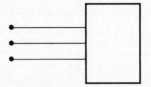

CONTENTS

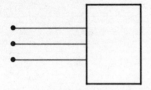

ACKNOWLEDGEMENTS

This book has been developed over a period of four years, in which time I have accumulated many debts of gratitude.

I am happy now to be able to express publicly my thanks to all of those who gave of their time in interviews and correspondence in the course of my research, and all those friends and colleagues at both Sheffield and Hull who have offered encouragement and support.

In particular, I must thank Professor Norman Lewis, whose scholarship, and whose personal interest in my research, has made this work possible.

I extend my thanks also to the University of Sheffield, for financial support during my doctoral research, and the University of Hull for funding research assistance in the summer of 1993.

I must also recognize the work of Julia May, an able and enthusiastic research assistant, whose contributions to the later stages of the production of the typescript were invaluable.

Finally, two people deserve special mention, for without the patience, support and humour of Sally, my wife, and Anna, my daughter, this work would not have been completed.

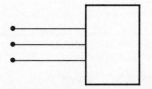

LIST OF ABBREVIATIONS

ACC	Association of County Councils
ACE	Advisory Centre on Education
AGM	Annual General Meeting
AMA	Association of Metropolitan Authorities
AMG	Annual Maintenance Grant
AMMA	Assistant Masters and Mistresses Association
CCTA	City College for the Technology of the Arts
CEO	Chief Education Officer
CIE	Choice in Education
CLA	Commissioner for Local Administration
CPS	Centre for Policy Studies
CPVE	Certificate of Pre-Vocational Education
CSE	Certificate of Secondary Education
CTC	City Technology College
DES	Department of Education and Science (*see also* DFE)
DFE	Department for Education (*see also* DES)
EA	Education Association
EOC	Equal Opportunities Commission
ERA	Education Reform Act 1988
FAS	Funding Agency for Schools
GCE	General Certificate of Education
GCSE	General Certificate of Secondary Education

GLC	Greater London Council
GM	grant maintained
GMSC	Grant Maintained Schools Centre
GMSF	Grant Maintained Schools Foundation
GMST	Grant Maintained Schools Trust
HMI	Her Majesty's Inspectorate
IEA	Institute of Economic Affairs
ILEA	Inner London Education Authority
INSET	In-Service Training
IPPR	Institute for Public Policy Research
LEA	Local Education Authority
LEAg	Local Education Agency
LMS	Local Management of Schools
LSI	Local Schools Information
MBC	Metropolitan Borough Council
MSC	Manpower Services Commission
NAGM	National Association of Governors and Managers
NAHT	National Association of Head Teachers
NASUWT	National Association of Schoolmasters and Union of Women Teachers
NCC	National Curriculum Council ('National Consumer Council' appears in full)
NUT	National Union of Teachers
Ofsted	Office for Standards in Education
PTA	parents–teachers association
QEB	Queen Elizabeth School for Boys, Barnet
SAC	Standing Advisory Committee (of Grant Maintained Schools)
SCAA	Schools Curriculum and Assessment Authority
SEAC	Schools Examination and Assessment Council
SED	Scottish Education Department (*see also* SOED)
SEN	Special Educational Needs
SG	Self-Governing
SGST	Self-Governing Schools Trust
SOED	Scottish Office Education Department (*see also* SED)
SPG	Special Purpose Grant
SPG(R)	Special Purpose Grant (Restructuring)
TEC	Training and Enterprise Council
TES	Times Educational Supplement
TVEI	Technical and Vocational Education Initiative

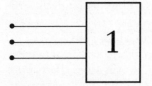

THE HISTORICAL CONTEXT: FROM BUTLER TO BAKER AND BEYOND

> The Education Reform Act of 1988 was the most important and far-reaching piece of educational law-making for England and Wales since the Education Act of 1944.
>
> Why? Because it altered the basic power structure of the education system.
>
> (Maclure, 1988, p. ix)

The role of the state is not constant. There are many descriptions of how the British state has altered in its functions and relationship with individuals over the last three hundred years and before. A brief and lucid version is given by Hill (1976) and takes the form of four phases.

It begins, in post-feudal times, with a model of a minimal state, with activities focused around defence, and the provision of sufficient stability and security to allow trade and commerce to develop and flourish; the state as facilitator. From then, as the imperialist era developed, and as urbanization rapidly took over, the state came to intervene more as a regulator of 'private' relationships, a role exemplified in the latter part of the nineteenth century by legislation relating to public health and employment. Gradually, the state is seen to add to these regulatory functions a new role as provider of services such as health care, housing and education, funded out of taxation. In modern times, especially following the Second World War, the state acquired a further involvement, as entrepreneur, controlling and managing key sectors of the economy as nationalized industries.

The justification for large-scale state intervention had been largely in terms of economic criteria, with government activity legitimated by reference to economic success. Thus, as world recession took over from the period of post-war economic growth, the British and other 'Western' governments were faced with what Habermas (1976) has described as a 'legitimation crisis'. The response of such governments was to seek a new basis for legitimacy, and this has resulted, largely within the last fifteen years, in a fifth phase, involving a marked reversal of state expansionism, typified by a process of privatization in all its manifestations, and a more general withdrawal of the state from many of the functions taken on in previous eras.

In line with this pattern of development, state intervention in education in Britain is a relatively recent phenomenon, with meaningful involvement dating only from the mid-nineteenth century, and the modern era of active state control beginning only in 1902. As with other areas of British life, the state's involvement in education can be said to have peaked in the period after 1944, with expansion of educational provision, predominantly under state control, reflecting general post-war economic growth.

This book is concerned with the reform of schooling initiated in England and Wales by the Education Reform Act 1988 (ERA), located firmly within the modern period of a remodelling of the state along minimalist lines. The central concepts to be considered, accountability and choice, are suggested by the reforms themselves, and perhaps even more by the associated rhetoric of the market. It is an attempt to assess how far the rhetoric is matched by empirical reality, and to assess the extent to which the delivery of state schooling, a crucial social service, fulfils constitutional expectations.

In carrying out such a task, it is essential that modern and current developments are viewed in their historical context. The author is, however, neither an educationist nor a historian, but a lawyer.

The law is implicated in the administration of education in a number of different ways. It is used as an instrument for implementing government policy, as a mechanism of challenge and accountability, and as such a source of legitimacy for administrative action, controlling executive discretion, and, perhaps most obviously, as a means of dispute resolution between competing individuals or groups *inter se*, or in relation to the state.

This book attempts to integrate a study of current issues in education administration with a consideration of their constitutional impact and is written from a 'public law' perspective that emphasizes the breadth of the presence and roles of 'law', rather than pursuing the predominant British legal academic tradition of cataloguing the detail of statute and case law.

Thus, one central theme of this work is the effectiveness or otherwise of mechanisms said to ensure the accountability, and hence legitimacy, of decision makers in state education. Such a theme remains of equally vital importance whether decisions are taken within a model based around bureaucratic planning or one in which quasi-market forces predominate. What emerges from a consideration of this theme is that we are not faced with a simple choice between central planning and unconstrained market forces. As is demonstrated in this book, even within the market model introduced by ERA and subsequent legislations significant regulatory, planning and other decision-making powers remain, although they have now been relocated. The need for such powers to be subject to adequate mechanisms of accountability also remains, whoever is exercising such powers.

The book is informed by a belief that the objectives of a system of state schooling should include equity in the distribution of this 'public good'. Thus, another recurrent theme is the tension between individual and collective goals in education administration, and the potential that exists for reinforcing, replicating or introducing hierarchy within our state school system.

In pursuit of these themes, in Chapter 2, an exploration of the concepts and themes at the heart of recent educational debate is undertaken. In Chapter 3, concrete manifestations of the recent reforms, as revealed by empirical inquiries into the schools' system, are discussed. In Chapter 4, developments are viewed specifically in the context of the role of the law, before an overview is taken, and conclusions reached in Chapter 5.

This first, largely descriptive, chapter sets out to establish the historical context in which recent developments must be viewed, and to introduce some of the themes which will be considered, both from a theoretical perspective and in light of empirical evidence, in later chapters.

FROM CONSENSUS TO CONFLICT?

The 1944 settlement

The White Paper, *Educational Reconstruction* (DFE, 1943), published in July 1943, stated as the objectives of the public education enterprise,

> to secure for children a happier childhood and a better start in life; to ensure a fuller measure of education and opportunity for young people and to provide means for all of developing the various talents with which they are endowed and so enriching the inheritance of the country whose citizens they are.

The Education Act 1944, which followed from the White Paper, is considered by most commentators to be the most important landmark in the administration of education in twentieth-century Britain – at least, that is, until 1988.

Under the terms of the 1944 Act, education was to be provided free of charge, to all children, from age five to 15. Though the Act established for the first time a national Ministry of Education, replacing the Board that had existed since 1899, it was clearly envisaged that the key body in achieving its educational aims was to be the Local Education Authorities (LEAs) which acquired wide-ranging duties and powers. Section 7 laid down a general principle that,

> The statutory system of public education shall be organised in three progressive stages to be known as primary education, secondary education, and further education; and it shall be the duty of the local education authority for every area, so far as their powers extend, to contribute towards the spiritual, moral, mental and physical development of the community by securing that efficient education throughout those stages shall be available to meet the needs of the population of their area.

The 1944 Act established a foundation for the educational edifice, but, as is typical of legislation in many areas of public administration in Britain, left large and crucial areas of the educational structure to be developed through secondary legislation, administrative action, and informal relationships, in this case between central government, local administrators, and education professionals.

The Act did not set out what was to be taught in schools. Though it was required that religious instruction be given at all maintained schools, the secular curriculum was to be determined at a local level. In practice, at least for the first 25 years following the Act, the responsibility for determining the curriculum fell largely on individual headteachers and other senior staff, who in turn were influenced by the requirements of external examinations (General Certificate of Education (GCE), Certificate of Secondary Education (CSE) and later the General Certificate of Secondary Education (GCSE)) established by the university-based examination boards. Teaching staff relied to varying extents on specialist curriculum advice provided by LEA advisers and Her Majesty's Inspectorate officers (HMIs). As recently as 1982, a Chief Education Officer (CEO) was able to state that 'within reasonable limits the headmaster and his staff are free to run the school as they think best, and to have the sort of curriculum they think best', leading to the conclusion that 'Most LEAs . . . still appear to value institutional discretion' (Bush and Kogan, 1982).

Though clearly providing the potential for discrepancies in what was taught both between and within LEAs, the system allowed scope for the development of new subject areas and teaching methods in response to specific local requirements. Indeed, from 1944 until the 1970s it was relatively rare for the DES to instigate changes in classroom practice on a national basis. Kogan (1978, p. 122) states that, 'an essential point about the development of education policy is that whilst many of the issues have been clarified and determined at the centre . . . many policies and practices have developed in the schools and the LEAs.'

However, Circulars and Guidance from the Ministry following the Act encouraged LEAs to develop a selective secondary system, which required a selection test at age 11 (the '11-plus') the result of which determined which branch of a differentiated secondary system the child would enter. Secondary schools were divided into 'grammar schools', 'technical schools' and 'secondary modern schools', though in many areas technical schools existed only briefly if at all.

The three types of school were intended by the architects of the Act to be of equal esteem though with different curricula emphases. In practice, the grammar schools with their emphasis on traditional subjects, their highly academic approach, and the success of their pupils in gaining places in higher education proved to be considered far more desirable by both parents and employers, and a hierarchy of state schools rapidly developed. The inevitable consequence of this was that the outcome of the 11-plus test came to be seen as crucial to the likelihood of a successful secondary school career, and the debate over the desirability of selective entry into secondary education, as opposed to a unitary comprehensive secondary system, proved to be the major education policy issue in Britain from the 1950s to the 1970s.

While the typology of controlled schools was established by the Act, the actual management of the local school system was put very firmly in the hands of the LEAs, to be constituted by the locally elected County and District Councils, though in practice, as the CEO quoted by Bush and Kogan, above, suggests, the practical arrangements allowed substantial flexibility to individual schools. LEAs were given general duties and powers to provide sufficient schools and to establish and maintain them, together with the ability to appoint and dismiss staff (Education Act 1944, Sections 8 and 9). Over all the LEA duties hung the power given to the Minister (later 'Secretary of State') under Section 99, to act in default of the failure by an authority to fulfil any duty imposed by the Act. The Minister also had power, under Section 68, to intervene and prevent an authority from acting 'unreasonably', as interpreted by the courts in cases such as those discussed in Chapter 4. The powers of the Minister to intervene, though clearly substantial, were in practice exercised relatively infrequently, and, despite the potential for indirect central government intervention in local authority business, including education, especially via financial measures (Harden, 1990), the management of maintained schools, both individually and collectively, lay essentially with the LEAs.

In order to carry out their general duties, the local authorities were also given more specific powers allowing them to control the opening, modification or closure of county schools (later modified by Sections 12–14 of the Education Act 1980) though plans in such cases were to be published and an opportunity given for objections to be made. Here again, the Minister was empowered to overturn such plans, but the power was used sparingly and the initiative in planning a local education system rested firmly with the LEA.

But, the 1944 Act had not only given LEAs the power to organize the numbers and types of schools within their area; it also gave the Authorities a consequential ability to, on occasions, override the wishes of individual parents.

The wishes of parents regarding choice of school for their children were to be taken into account, but, by virtue of Section 76, only 'so far as is compatible with the provision of efficient instruction and training and the avoidance of unreasonable expenditure', and the principle of selection by ability and aptitude into grammar schools remained. The element of discretion in relation to parental wishes granted to LEAs under Section 76, confirmed by the courts in cases such as *Watt v Kesteven* ([1955] 1 QB 408) and *Cumings v Birkenhead* ([1972] Ch. 12), combined with the more general power to reorganize schooling in an area, and only infrequent use of powers of intervention by Ministers, to allow LEAs to plan and manage pupil numbers and admission levels across all their schools in pursuit of efficient and economic schooling while fulfilling their general duty to provide sufficient suitable school places.

The 1950s and 1960s – expansion and changes of focus

While in the 1950s educationists had placed great emphasis on issues arising out of the tripartite system, and particularly the question of access to grammar school places, by the 1960s the focus was switching inside schools, away from the system as a whole, with the examination of causes of 'working-class failure' becoming a central issue. Labour/Fabian thinking was now largely expressed in terms of access to the occupational hierarchy, or 'educational outcome', a 'harder' concept of equality than hitherto, with a push towards comprehensivization being seen as the chief egalitarian weapon. The Plowden Report (DFE, 1967) proposed 'educational priority areas' as a forward step towards greater equality. In effect, positive discrimination was suggested to address in-built disadvantages, especially for racial minority groups.

Most writers identify a broad consensus in educational thought and policy making around and following the 1944 Act, at least until the late 1950s or early 1960s. Though distinct tensions can be seen throughout the intervening period, and indeed it is possible to construct a persuasive conflict-based model (Salter and Tapper, 1981), most commentators tend not to present conflict as the dominant model until the mid-1970s.

EDUCATION AND SOCIAL POLICY

Some of the central themes in education policy making through the 1944–75 period have already been touched upon above.

Lawson and Silver (1973, p. 421) state that,

> The educational reforms which were to take effect from 1945 were intended to remove some of the stigmas attached to lower-class education, provide a new pattern of opportunity, and set education in a framework of improved welfare and social justice.

The consensus around meritocratic principles that resulted in the establishment of the post-1944 tripartite system largely masked the availability of a variety of policy options. However, following the Crowther Report (DFE, 1959) and Newsom Report (DFE, 1963), an increased awareness of the relevance of environmental factors to any notional equality of opportunity caused a re-examination of the principles underlying the 1944 settlement.

Labour's adoption of a definite and more active policy in favour of comprehensivization, and the Plowden Report (DFE, 1967), gave a stronger voice to an alternative view, involving a 'harder' concept of equality (equality of outcome) rather than the traditional view of equality as equality of opportunity.

Finch (1984) locates the 1944 Act within a collectivist and pro-egalitarian 'spirit of the age' arising out of the war. She observes that R.A. Butler, chief architect of the 1944 Act accepted that the egalitarian principles within the Act could be undermined by general social inequalities, implying that more substantive equality would require a broader programme of social engineering.

Finch examines the ways in which education policy has been implemented and justified in the post-war period up to 1984, and notes a central tension between policy arguments seeking to further the interests of individual children, and those aimed primarily at benefits for 'society', and more specifically, the particular needs of a developing and changing capitalist economy. She goes on to find that,

> measures designed for the benefit of the recipients seem likely to attract significant support from state funding only if they are also promoting some other kind of interest which derives from a 'society's benefit' rather than an 'individual's benefit' rationale.
>
> (Finch, 1984, p. 110)

She goes on to state that education as social policy reflects social, economic and political life, which, writing in 1984, she believed was illustrated 'in a more explicit linking of education to the economy and in certain changes of emphasis within the curriculum' as supported by what she called the 'radical right'.

It should be clear from what has gone before that policy formation in the 1944–75 period, and indeed beyond, took place on at least four levels: central government, LEA, individual institution, and, teachers, both collectively and individually. Despite the fact that most commentators refer to 'partnership' and 'consensus' in describing the arrangements for the establishment and administration of education policy in the post-war years, it is clear that educational policy can also be portrayed as a contested arena, with any consensual agreement being only at the level of the lowest common denominator. The account given by Salter and Tapper (1981) in their search for the 'social dynamic of change' in education administration, suggests strongly that the education bureaucracy, and in particular the DES, has been capable of self-generation and controlling the direction of education to a much greater degree than is often allowed for. In general, however, evidence suggests that if any meaningful consensus did ever exist it suffered a terminal breakdown some time around the mid-1970s, the period in which the influence of trade unions began its steep and long decline, with the increased use and impact of litigation (Milman, 1986) and imposition of control by legal rules in this area being symptomatic of its demise.

Despite political tensions, Kogan noted in 1978 that 'over the years, conventions and understandings about the relationships between central government, the local authorities and schools, and about the freedom allowed institutional practitioners, have been confirmed and extended'. He refers to 'powerful and consensual continuities', operating within the large realm of freedom existing within the legislative framework.

The 1970s – contraction and conflict

With the start of the 1970s, came the end of the post-war expansion in British education, and the start of an attack on public expenditure and a general trend towards the contraction of state provision.

Bush and Kogan (1982, p. 61) state that,

> The precise point in time when expansion gave way to a steady state or reduction is open to debate, but in 1970 the number of pupils and teachers in the system were still growing and administrators still sought to provide enough accommodation for increasing demand. By the end of the decade, contraction dominated educational planning.

At the same time, egalitarianism began to lose its central place in the educational debates of the 1970s. While the left began to focus on education as a form of social control in the service of capitalism, the right increasingly emphasized questions of content and standards, with the series of Black Papers from 1969 onwards proving influential, and, beginning to change the nature of the debate.

Significant changes in the location of power in educational policy making were also taking place. Kogan (1978) comments that central government influence largely took the form of guidance, example and encouragement during the expansionist era, but became increasingly prescriptive as contraction and financial stringency took over. By the early 1980s, when Bush and Kogan (1982) carried out their survey of changing roles of CEOs, following up *County Hall* (Kogan and Van der Eyken, 1973), they found that, 'In the past it could be assumed that CEOs were among the main agents of change. In the period that we describe he emerges at least as much as the recipient as the promoter of the main changes' (p. 61).

Their respondents commented on central government influence being directly exerted via legislation on education policy (e.g. the requirement to develop comprehensive policies in the 1976 Act), but also general restrictions imposed on local authority spending (e.g. Local Government Planning and Land Act 1980), and some were already noticing increases in central influence over the curriculum.

They found that the realm of the 'educational establishment' was under threat from central government initiatives, and, that the balance of power had already shifted, so that the CEO was, arguably, no longer at the centre of the 'web of relations'. The CEOs' power had been challenged not only by central government, but also by trends towards corporate management in local government. The increased use in this period of litigation to resolve disputes is indicative of the breakdown of existing relationships.

Within the legislative framework for education there is clearly potential for policy differences to arise, and, while in judicial review actions the courts are theoretically confined to considering how a decision has been arrived at rather than its merits, the courts have on occasion acted in such a way as to substantially affect the policy-making process. Kogan (1978) and other commentators note an increased use of the law through the 1960s and 1970s to resolve disputes which could be viewed as largely matters of educational policy.

Secondary reorganization plans in Enfield in 1967 saw the courts intervening to ensure that both the LEA and the Secretary of State followed minimum required consultation procedures (*Lee v DES* ([1967] 66 LGR 195), *Bradbury v Enfield LBC* ([1967] 3 All ER 434), while the case of *Secretary of State for Education and Science v Metropolitan Borough of Tameside* ([1976] 3 WLR 641 HL) considered in Chapter 4, is of substantial legal, if not necessarily educational, significance.

The arrival of a Conservative government in 1970, and the resulting slowing down of comprehensivization caused the system and the abolition of the '11-plus' to be implemented unevenly.

In response to the court's decision in Tameside, the Labour government introduced the Education Act 1976, giving the Secretary of State the means to require LEAs to take steps towards the introduction of comprehensive secondary schooling. However, even after this Act LEA reorganizations proceeded on a piecemeal basis, and the election of a Conservative central government in 1979 effectively ended for the immediate future questions of a comprehensive policy being forcibly imposed from the centre.

Comprehensive systems were and still are applied unevenly across the country, though Sharp and Dunford (1990) indicate that by the mid-1980s the majority of secondary pupils in the public sector were in comprehensive schools. Patterns of comprehensivization largely reflect the political stand-point of the relevant LEAs, despite the wishes or efforts of central government. The question of retaining grammar school status in the face of LEA plans to reorganize, or on occasions the wish to remain as a comprehensive school within an LEA committed to a system based on grammar schools, has proved to be a key factor in the decision of a number of schools to apply under ERA to opt-out of LEA control to grant-maintained status.

Despite this potential for uncertainty and inconsistency and the long-running debate over comprehensivization, the thirty-year period after the 1944 Act was largely a period of educational growth and relative calm in which the LEA generally exercised the greatest influence on policy in its locality. However, from the mid-1970s, open conflict over educational policy, and a more overt power struggle become apparent.

Most commentators refer to the then Prime Minister James Callaghan's speech at Ruskin College in October 1976, as launching what became known as 'The Great Debate' on education in Britain. However, by the time of Callaghan's Ruskin speech, three themes had already begun to dominate the educational debate and were reflected in the Prime Minister's comments: the content of education, the relationship of education to the economy and in particular questions over whether education was 'failing' industry, and, though this was rather a creeping phenomenon until the late 1980s, the increasing influence of central government over education. Chitty (1989) identifies the Ruskin speech as significant in that it made clear, 'at the very highest political level', that the era of educational expansion was at an end.

The increasing scale of unemployment amongst the young throughout the 1970s and 1980s later led to much more discussion, often dominated by the political right, on the role of education in society. Groups on the right-wing of the Conservative Party were able to capitalize on the issues acknowledged in the Ruskin speech, many already having been discussed in the Black Papers, and the concern arising out of specific cases such as William Tyndale School (ILEA, 1976) to form the basis for the Thatcher reforms of education which culminated in ERA.

The Taylor Report

The Taylor Committee was established in 1975 to consider lay participation in education, as a response to the general 'consumer movement', and says Maclure, specifically pressure from the National Association of Governors and Managers (NAGM). The Taylor Report (DFE, 1977) brought onto the agenda a more representative basis and active role for governing bodies, which, as we shall see, was to be pursued actively by the Conservative governments of the 1980s.

The 1944 Act provided a statutory foundation for the position of governing bodies for individual schools. In voluntary aided schools, the governing body would carry a majority of members appointed by the relevant religious or charitable body, while county schools would have a majority of LEA appointed governors. Although the spirit of the Act, and of the 1944 White Paper, *Principles of Government* (DFE, 1944), seems to be that school governing bodies should play an active role in the running of individual schools, their actual role varied widely from area to area. Though governing bodies would on occasion have serious matters to consider (for example a disciplinary matter relating to teaching staff, or if the school's future was under threat), governors' duties would often be little more than ceremonial. Howell (1981, p. 194) notes that

> Sceptics doubted whether there was any real justification for schemes of government which could be expensive, time-consuming, irritating and essentially fruitless. There was a sense in which the governors were a fifth wheel on the coach.

Bush and Kogan (1982) note that CEOs interviewed by them had observed a slight increase in activity generated by governing bodies over the preceding ten years, and that the CEOs had come to accept that governors had a role to play in the system, though one which was largely undefined.

The Taylor Committee recommended that school governing bodies should exert considerably more influence than hitherto over the running of schools, with significantly increased powers delegated to governing bodies by the LEA. The Report also recommended that each school should have its own governing body, and that there should be equal representation of each of four constituencies: LEAs, staff, parents and the community.

The proposals met with substantial opposition, from many LEAs and teachers, and although the Labour government's Education Bill in 1978 did seek to establish governing bodies for all schools, it was proposed that the Secretary of State would have the power to set, by Regulation, the precise composition of governing bodies.

However, neither the proposals in the Bill, or the associated White Paper on the composition of governing bodies proposals ever obtained legal force.

The 1979 General Election produced a victory for the Conservatives, led by former Secretary of State for Education, Margaret Thatcher, and marked the start of a new era in the relationship between law and education policy.

THE THATCHERITE AGENDA

Introduction

The Education Reform Act 1988 (ERA) is the most wide-ranging piece of legislation on the subject of education since the landmark Education Act 1944. Both the 1944 Act and ERA can be viewed in essence as attempts, via the introduction and exercise of legal powers, to shape the world of education in England and Wales so as to fit into a broader model of society. Like the 1944 Act, ERA can be seen as representative of the nationally dominant political ideals and policy preferences of its time.

ERA, like other major pieces of legislation of the Thatcher period, as part of the remodelling of the state, challenged the established practices and power relationships within the area of public sector activity, though clearly the agenda had already been partially shaped under Callaghan's Labour administration.

Legislation on social policy issues under the Thatcher administrations contained certain recurrent and typical themes. Central/local government relations were altered, in such a way as to reduce the discretionary powers of local authorities, restricting the powers of local government through requirements of primary and secondary legislation made by central government, such as the introduction of Compulsory Competitive Tendering. At the same time, new regulatory arrangements were introduced into many areas of traditional public sector activity, with an intended consequence of bringing competition into what were considered monopoly areas. This can be viewed as symptomatic of a broad philosophical position which favours withdrawal of the state from certain functions, including some regulatory roles, in order to further the role of market forces.

A third key strand of social policy legislation in the 1980s was to stress a transfer of power to individuals, as 'consumers', and away from public bodies. The most obvious examples of this are the reforms of the National Health Service (NHS), and ERA, where a dissemination of power is claimed to have taken place, from the traditional establishments which plan and manage these public services, into the hands of individual medical practices and units, and, in the world of education, to parents and individual schools. Power is claimed to have shifted from service provider to service user. 'Choice' for individuals or 'purchasers' is said to have been increased, and 'accountability' of the service 'providers' enhanced (cf. Longley, 1993).

The remainder of this section is concerned with the genesis and theoretical underpinnings of these developments in relation to state schooling.

The first two Thatcher administrations

Knight (1990) sees the 1979 Cabinet as an uneasy mix of the old paternalist wing of the Conservative Party and the new 'economic Thatcherite' wing. He notes that the appointment of Mark Carlisle as Secretary of State in preference to supporters of the 'social market' and education vouchers such as Rhodes Boyson effectively left education in the hands of the older school of Toryism.

The early education legislation (Education Acts 1979, 1980 and 1981) of the first Thatcher government gave little indication of the radical reform to come. Of particular relevance is the 1980 Act, which although apparently intended to enhance parental choice of school was a disappointment to those within the Conservative Party who sought the introduction of a system of school 'vouchers', a concept discussed further in Chapter 2.

As stated earlier, Section 76 of the 1944 Act had allowed LEAs a significant degree of discretion to override the wishes of individual parents as to which school their child should attend. In explicitly requiring LEAs to allow parents to express a preference (Section 6(1)), and requiring the LEA to admit the child to the chosen school (Section 6(2)), the 1980 Act superficially gives the appearance of reversing the balance of power. However, LEAs were not obliged to comply with parental preference if they could establish one of the exceptions set out in Section 6(3). Of these exceptions, the widest and most significant was Section 6(3)(a), which allowed the LEA not to comply with parental preference 'if compliance with the preference would prejudice the provision of efficient education or the efficient use of resources'. Adler *et al.* (1989) point towards the breadth of this exception in practice, and note the relative weakness of parental choice granted under the 1980 Act for England and Wales when compared to the position north of the border under the Education (Scotland) Act 1981 (see Chapters 2 and 3).

The 1980 Act did however provide, at least in theory, a further bolster to parental choice in the form of statutory appeals committees to be established by LEAs to deal with admission and exclusion appeals, replacing the common but ill-defined and *ad hoc* non-statutory appeals procedures previously established by many LEAs (Lewis and Birkinshaw, 1979).

Parental choice was already becoming a strong theme in Conservative education policy, and the focus on this aspect of parental involvement, despite the many other potential forms of enhancing parental influence in schools (Partington and Wragg, 1989; Templeton, 1989), was to become the single track approach to parental empowerment, resulting in a polarization of the issues of choice and planning.

However, in the early 1980s, educational change was neither radical nor rapid. Though extensive discussion of the education service took place from 1981–6, and indeed there was widespread industrial action by teachers, resulting ultimately in the Teachers Pay and Conditions Act 1987, the agenda was still very much based around the themes established by Callaghan in his Ruskin College speech.

Even so, Sharp and Dunford (1990) believe that it was during the first half of the 1980s that 'the balance of power in the control of education was subtly moved from the LEAs to central government and to individual schools'.

The 1985 White Paper (DFE, 1985) and Education (No. 2) Act 1986 again addressed the role and composition of governing bodies, building on the concept of elected parent governors first introduced in the 1980 Act, but not going as far as to give parents a majority on governing bodies.

However, perhaps of more significance in this period is an increasing degree of intervention by central government in education administration, and a consequent narrowing of the discretion available to LEAs (Riley, 1992). Bush *et al.* (1989) note not only a heightened level of intervention, but also that initiatives such as In-Service Training (INSET) funding, Manpower Services Commission (MSC) managed projects such as the Technical and Vocational Training Initiative (TVEI), and control of general local government expenditure introduced in this period reflect also a movement of power over the education purse away not only from LEAs, but also the Department of Education and Science (DES), a trend continued, as Riley (1992) notes, by the development of Training and Enterprise Councils (TECs), in which the influence of LEAs can be marginalized. As Chitty (1989) notes in relation to the City Technology College (CTC) programme under ERA, in addition to education-related initiatives from other central government departments, the role of Margaret Thatcher's Downing Street Policy Unit in the formulation of education policies should not be underestimated.

A genuinely Thatcherite prescription

Maclure (1988), considers that, prior to the mid-1970s, 'The belief that education is a self-justifying good was an article of faith not a tentative hypothesis', and suggests that 'Perhaps it is the loss of this faith which separates the educational discourse of the 1980s most sharply from that of the earlier period.' Discussing the proliferation of right-wing education think-tanks in the 1970s and 1980s, he notes that, 'Part of the story is about bringing views which were once regarded as unacceptable into common currency. In this way, the Right changed the boundaries of the debate.'

Even though it could be claimed that the discourse was changing from the mid-1970s onwards, it was still not possible for the Conservative government to introduce radical reforms of education until the late 1980s, when the 'New Right' had won the ideological battle within the Conservative Party.

This struggle is characterized in its simplest form by Brown (1989) as between the 'Free Marketeers' and the 'Authoritarian Right'. Dale (1983) identifies a decisive move under Thatcher's leadership away from the hitherto dominant influence of the Old Tories, typified by Edward Heath's benevolent paternalism, in the tradition of Disraeli's 'one nation'. The new dominant force, Thatcherism, is seen by Dale as a distillate of the views of a number of strands of Conservative thinking, including the populists, moral entrepreneurs and the privatizers. In a later work Dale (1989) refers to Stuart Hall's use of the term 'authoritarian populism' to describe this phenomenon which Dale states, 'both draws on selectively and recombines existing strands of conservatism . . . and it loosely knits these together with opportunistic reactions to contemporary problems'. Inevitably, the diverse nature of the views incorporated into Thatcherism result in readily observable ongoing tensions and internal inconsistencies within this 'philosophy'.

There is no doubt that Sir Keith Joseph had sought to inject market forces into education during his period in office at DES which started in 1981, and was attracted by the replacement of a planning model for education administration with one that better fitted the government's preferred economic model. Maclure (1988) states that the enhancement of parental choice via the device of 'education vouchers' (discussed further in Chapter 2) was Joseph's first and dominant priority during his early period in office at the DES; but that he was persuaded by civil servants that the practical difficulties of introducing such a system were insuperable. Knight (1990) is unsure whether the absence of a proposal for vouchers in the 1983 Conservative Manifesto was due to an ideological victory for the centralists, or whether, more simply, the financial cost of introducing a scheme was ultimately considered too high.

The conclusion reached by Chitty (1989, p. 199) on Joseph's failure to proceed with education vouchers is that, 'It may be that he was defeated by his own civil servants; or it may be, as Wilby has suggested, that he was unable to find ways of achieving his objectives that would satisfy his own need for coherent solutions to problems.' Chitty contrasts Joseph's concern with intellectual coherence with the approach of his successor, Kenneth Baker. He quotes a description of Baker as 'the supreme pragmatist'. Knight (1990, p. 179) comments that,

the appointment of Kenneth Baker as the new Education Secretary on 21st May 1986 suggested tactical skill and administrative ability in the presentation of Conservative educational reforms were considered greater attributes for securing electoral success than the talent to initiate policy itself.

The Conservative manifestos on education for the 1979 and 1983 general elections promised little in the way of radical change; indeed Chitty is able to quote Thatcher in 1987 as regretting earlier failures to tackle the ills of the public education system. Chitty believes that the real break came in 1987. Although Whitty and Menter (1989) place the end of the first phase of Thatcherite education policy a little earlier, around 1985 or 1986, there can be no doubt that by 1987, a genuinely Thatcherite prescription for education had finally emerged. Indeed, Chitty (1989) suggests that ERA, as introduced by Kenneth Baker, allowed a system of education vouchers to be introduced into public education 'under a different name'.

The form ERA ultimately took appears to have been the result of the congeries of potentially contradictory concepts addressed in the publications of the various right-wing think-tanks. The conflicting pressures from various branches of the Conservative Party, typically characterized as the neo-liberal and neo-conservative, are apparent in the contradictions and conflict within, and arising from, ERA discussed in the wake of the Act by various commentators (Bash and Coulby, 1989; Lawton, 1989; Flude and Hammer, 1990).

On this occasion, as Maclure comments, the government avoided any risk of the chosen policy being scuppered by those outside the inner circle – the fate, many believe of the voucher scheme pursued by Joseph:

> What eventually emerged in the election manifesto – and therefore ultimately in the Act – was assembled in secret in the nine months before the 1987 General Election. There was a determined effort not to consult either the DES or the civil servants or chief education officers or local politicians. Under the discreet eye of Brian Griffiths, head of the Prime Minister's Policy Unit, the outline of a radical reform was set down in bold lines from which there was no going back. The transition from 1944 to 1988 was complete: so complete that there was no longer any need to seek consensus.
>
> (Maclure, 1988, p. 166)

THE RELOCATION OF POWER

From Bill to Act

Following the Conservative election victory, the announcement that legislation reforming education was to be introduced was made in the Queen's Speech on 17 June 1987.

The legislative process began with the publication of the various consultation documents by DES, of which the most controversial, on the National Curriculum, was published in July. Only four months later, a period which included the school 'summer shutdown', the Bill was presented to the Commons for First Reading.

Criticism of the lack of depth of consultation, and unfavourable comparisons with the process that resulted in the 1944 Act came from both within and outside Parliament. The collection of materials presented by Haviland (1988) demonstrates, however, that numerous bodies did manage to produce considered and clear responses despite the pressure of time. What is equally clear from Haviland's work is that the exercise was largely futile, as the government chose to ignore the mass of overwhelmingly critical responses.

Similar criticisms in relation to the speed the Bill was forced through Parliament are highlighted by Simon (1988). Indeed, an examination of the Official Report of the Debates and Committee proceedings show that no changes were made that affected the substance of the Bill. The Conservative government's elected majority in the Commons, with the resulting in-built majority in Committee, and their willingness to exploit their majority in the Lords, by bringing in large numbers of hereditary peers when necessary, combined with the ruthless use of guillotines to impose strict limits on both the quantity and effectiveness of debate.

Opening the Second Reading debate in the Commons on 1 December 1987, Kenneth Baker, the then Secretary of State for Education and Science, used language typical of the Bill's supporters. He talked of 'consumers' of education, of 'freeing' schools and colleges, and 'increasing choice and freedom'.

Jack Straw, Labour's spokesperson on education, pointed towards the consensual nature of Butler's 1944 Act, and the concept of egalitarianism underlying that Act, which he contrasted with Baker having told the Conservative Party conference in October 1987 that, 'the pursuit of egalitarianism is over'. Straw went on to refer to 175 new powers which he claimed were being placed in the hands of the Secretary of State, and, quoting comments from the Institute of Economic Affairs, talked of 'a frightening degree of secondary legislation and bureaucracy for years ahead'.

Labour combined with Liberal Democrat and Plaid Cymru members both on the floor of the House and in Committee, though, perhaps inevitably, press coverage focused on former Conservative Prime Minister Edward Heath's attack on his party's attempt to centralize power. He commented that,

> The Secretary of State has taken more power under this Bill than any other member of the cabinet. The extent of the Secretary of State's power will be overwhelming. Within the Parliamentary system, no Secretary of State should ever be allowed to hold such a degree of power.
> (Hansard, Commons, Vol. 123, Col. 792)

The Bill went on to Standing Committee where, as Simon (1988) comments, 'not a single concession of any importance was made'.

The Report Stage and Third Reading Debate saw little new, though Secretary of State Baker stated that he 'would find it constitutionally unacceptable for the [Secretary of State] to impose his own national curriculum'. Interventions by subsequent holders of that office, particularly during the tenure of Kenneth Clarke, raise significant questions as to whether Baker's successors consider themselves bound by these sentiments.

The main thrusts of parliamentary opposition to the Bill are summarized in a passage from a speech by Liberal Democrat leader Paddy Ashdown:

> The Bill has been founded on ideology rather than good sense and has been informed throughout by a sense of vindictiveness against teachers, local government, LEAs, ILEA and all those tribal enemies of the Conservative Party. That is what underpins the Bill . . . The secret aims of the Bill are to diminish the power of local government, to centralise the power over education in the hands of the Secretary of State and to reinforce privilege in our education system.
>
> (Hansard, Commons, Vol. 130, Col. 810)

What concessions that were made by the government came in the course of the Bill's passage through the Lords, where powerful coalitions forced some amendments on higher education and others to protect the position of Special Educational Needs (SEN) statemented pupils. A limited compromise on religious education, and a minor concession on the opt-out ballot process also resulted.

Ultimately, the enormous Bill emerged from the parliamentary process to gain Royal Assent on 27 July 1988 very much in the form it had gone in. The principle features of the legislation remained unchanged, with little scope for effective opposition having been allowed by the government's ruthless management of the Bill.

ERA – the relocation of power

The content of ERA is well-documented elsewhere; in particular, Maclure (1988) provides a useful commentary on the provisions and their implications. In the next few pages I wish only to highlight certain central aspects of ERA that are of particular significance for my major themes of choice and accountability, and must, within the compass of this work, assume that readers have a working knowledge of the nature of the ERA reforms. An examination of the underlying concepts is undertaken in Chapter 2.

In essence, the relocation of power under ERA has been in two directions. While certain measures have the stated intention of decentralizing, or disseminating power, from the LEAs to individual schools, and to parents as 'consumers', other measures have the result of centralizing power, at the Department for Education (DFE).

The stated intention of the government was to introduce, via the decentralizing measures, a substantial element of competition between schools, with the result of increasing, via market pressures, accountability in the management of schools, which would, it was claimed, lead to enhanced educational standards. Meanwhile, by centralizing power, especially in relation to the curriculum, consistency in what was offered to children would be improved, and most importantly, by standardizing assessment procedures and publishing results in such a way as to enable comparisons to be made between schools, would enable parents to make informed choices between schools, again, with the claimed end product of improved accountability and educational standards. A detailed consideration of the relationship between accountability, choice and standards is undertaken in the next chapter, and empirical evidence as to the outcomes of the reforms is presented in Chapter 3; for the moment, it is necessary only to indicate the form that the reforms took, in order to facilitate the later discussion.

Decentralization

The decentralizing measures in the ERA fall into two main groups. First, there are those provisions relating to open enrolment and Local Management of Schools (LMS). In essence, these measures provide the primary motive force for competition, so central to the ERA's purpose.

Under open enrolment, LEAs lose the power to restrict admissions to schools in pursuit of policy aims, or in response to demographic changes. Henceforth, schools must in effect admit up to their physical capacity. Thus, it is no longer possible for LEAs to restrict admissions to 'popular' schools in order to ensure admissions levels at less popular schools, or to plan admissions in the interests of economic or educational efficiency.

Under LMS the role of heads and governing bodies is expanded beyond recognition. In 1981, Fenwick and MacBride (1981) noted that the power of the LEA was then still 'formidable enough to ensure its ultimate constitutional supremacy in the locality', and although the 1986 (No. 2) Act amended the composition of governing bodies, and granted governors powers to consider the secular curriculum, and to determine a policy on sex education, while putting 'the conduct of the school' and responsibility for 'the determination and organisation of the secular curriculum' within the responsibility of the headteacher, it was the LEA that retained financial control over the school and responsibility for staffing matters. However, under Sections 31 to 51 of the ERA, the role of heads and governing bodies has been expanded to the extent that the LEA is left virtually without responsibility or power for the day-to-day running of maintained schools.

Each LEA was charged with establishing a formula, subject to approval by the Secretary of State, for the distribution of its school budget to the individual institutions, and the authority also remained responsible for providing a limited range of authority-wide services, and for certain inspection and advice functions, now further amended by the Education (Schools) Act 1992. However, all other management functions with regard to general expenditure, appointments and dismissals of staff, and, the delivery of the national curriculum are placed within the remit of the governing body and the headteacher.

The net effect of these measures is to establish the basis for a competitive market in schooling, enabling parents to choose between schools, and requiring schools to compete to attract pupils.

The second tranche of measures aimed at enhancing competition involves the creation of two new and highly controversial categories of schools. The process of opting-out, to grant maintained (GM) status, enables schools to opt-out of local authority control and instead to be funded directly by central government, and managed exclusively by their governing body, and issues relating to opting-out are dealt with at some length in Chapters 3 and 4. As will be demonstrated, even though opting-out has as yet occurred only on a small scale (less than 300 schools out of a possible 23,000 had opted out by early 1992) the impact of such moves has been wholly disproportionate to the scale of activity, fundamentally changing the nature of the administration of a local system of schools, and largely undermining the planning function of the LEA.

For the moment, it is sufficient to note that opting-out was supposed to represent an additional mechanism by which accountability and hence educational standards would be enhanced. Parents, if dissatisfied with management of the school under the LEA, could vote to change the management; the complacency of LEAs, and their local monopoly would be broken.

The second new category of schools is City Technology Colleges (CTCs) and City Colleges for the Technology of the Arts (CCTAs) (henceforth referred to generically as 'CTCs'). In contrast to the 52 sections of ERA required for the introduction of GM schools, CTCs were introduced by a single section, Section 105, which establishes the characteristics of these schools.

Section 105(2) states that they are to be in urban areas and provide education for 11–18 year-olds drawn mostly from the locality, and, in the case of CTCs have 'a broad curriculum with an emphasis on science and technology' while CCTAs must offer 'a broad curriculum with an emphasis . . . on technology in its application to the performing and creative arts'. The National Curriculum does not formally apply to CTCs. Section 105(3) empowers the Secretary of State to make payments towards both capital and current expenditure at these schools.

By the time the CTC concept was given legislative form, it had already changed significantly from its original shape. As the Bristol Polytechnic

Education Study Group state, 'the stress has changed to urban rather than inner city areas and the government has shown itself willing to provide up to 80 per cent of capital costs as well as 100 per cent of current expenditure (Bash and Coulby, 1989).

The originally expressed aim was that these colleges, free of the constraints of the National Curriculum, able to teach a broad curriculum with a particular emphasis, free to set their own conditions of service for teachers, and able to vary the length of the school day for pupils and so on, would become 'beacons of excellence'. They were to be funded predominantly by business sponsors, with the DES topping up the funding. In effect, CTCs were to provide a 'private' education (in the sense of being free of the constraints of state bureaucracy) funded largely by private money. However, sponsorships were both fewer and smaller than the government had hoped so, unwilling to allow the project to fail, the government has ended up providing the majority of capital and current expenditure, thus providing a 'private' education with 'public' money. The experiment was originally intended to produce a first wave of some 20 CTCs. However, it seems that Treasury pressure resulted in the curtailing of the experiment with only 15 CTCs established or awaiting completion.

Though neither GM schools nor CTCs as yet form a significant group of schools in relation to the overall numbers of existing state schools, both have proved attractive to parents, and have therefore had a considerable impact on the local schools 'market'. Though there is no evidence as yet to suggest that such schools have produced any enhancement in educational standards, there is no doubt that GM schools in particular form a central plank in the government's plans for the future administration of education, as demonstrated in the 1992 White Paper (DFE, 1992) discussed below.

Centralization

The key centralizing measure was contained in Sections 1 to 25 which enabled the Secretary of State to establish a national curriculum and associated testing arrangements.

As has been noted above, the settlement achieved under the 1944 Act did not impose a curriculum upon individual schools or LEAs. In practice, curricular decisions were largely taken locally, by education professionals in the form of senior staff at schools and local advisers and HMIs. Though central intervention from the DES increased through the 1980s, in the form of guidance through Circulars, and a national curriculum of some sort began to look increasingly likely, Maclure (1988) points out that as late as 1985 the official position as stated in Secretary of State Joseph's White Paper *Better Schools* (DFE, 1985) was 'that the government had no intention to introduce legislation redefining responsibility for the curriculum'.

However, following the replacement of Keith Joseph by Kenneth Baker, the Conservative Election Manifesto for 1987 demonstrated a clear commitment to a national curriculum. Duly returned to office in the June election, the introduction of the National Curriculum became and has remained perhaps the most controversial of the package of measures introduced in the ERA. The boycott by teachers in 1993 of the Key Stage 3 tests demonstrated an ongoing hostility within the teaching profession to the detail, if not necessarily the principle, of nationally orchestrated testing; for the first time since the mid-1980s, teachers combined to present effective opposition to central government policies.

The provisions of Sections 1–25 of the ERA fundamentally alter the decision-making process over curriculum content. The legislation provides a framework for the Secretary of State to make, by Order, detailed requirements regarding the curriculum, attainment targets, and methods of assessing children. In the exercise of these powers the Secretary of State is to be advised by newly created bodies, the National Curriculum Council (NCC) (and Curriculum Council for Wales) and Schools Examinations and Assessment Council (SEAC) (now to be amalgamated as the Schools Curriculum and Assessment Authority, SCAA). However, these bodies are to consist of appointees of the Secretary of State, and, though bound by requirements of consultation in respect of the exercise of some of these powers, the finality of the Secretary of State's decision remains. The Secretary of State is also empowered to determine appeals from parents who are dissatisfied with a school's 'delivery' of the National Curriculum. While power over the curriculum and testing arrangements rests with the Secretary of State, and the exercise of these powers has produced a plethora of statutory instruments and guidance, it is individual schools that are required to give effect to the prescribed curriculum and testing requirements.

Though the National Curriculum provides the most obvious example of centralization of power under the ERA, there can be little doubt that the introduction of GM schools and CTCs, which are to be approved and funded by central government, and the power for the Secretary of State to approve or reject LMS budgets, also represent significant increases in central control over the education system.

In passing, it should be noted that the ERA provided for the abolition of the Inner London Education Authority (ILEA) with effect from April 1990. ILEA's record of 'progressive' education and resistance to central government policy is well known; indeed, it represents a significant part of the folklore of the various British education cultures, of both political left and right. Its abolition by the ERA is perhaps not as surprising as its survival of the abolition of the GLC in 1985.

Upon the abolition of the directly elected ILEA, power and responsibility for educational provision passed to the individual London Boroughs. The life of the London Residuary Body (originally established as a consequence of the abolition of the GLC) was effectively extended to oversee the disposal of ILEA assets. Each Borough was obliged to develop strategic plans relating to education provision, with 'safety net' arrangements scheduled to exist until 1994/5. As Maclure (1988) commented, 'In the case of those boroughs which are themselves already rate-capped, the cuts in education have to be managed alongside cuts in all other services.'

Discussing the potential consequences of ILEA's abolition, Maclure (1988, p. 117) could see no educational benefits: 'It is difficult to forecast the impact of London reorganisation on the schools, the staff and governing bodies, except in terms of a catalogue of potential disasters in the short term, followed, at best, by a period of consolidation.' For the government, the abolition of ILEA must be considered a political victory, however, as Jones (1989) has observed, 'the educational issues that the ILEA posed for the state cannot, unlike the ILEA, be legislated away'.

AFTER ERA

1987–1993

There can be no doubt that the ERA represents the most significant relocation of power in the administration of education in England and Wales since 1944. It is therefore, perhaps surprising to find that an Act of such magnitude was followed not by a quiet period of 'bedding down', but instead by a period in which further significant developments have added unpredictable problems to the already immense task of implementing it.

One aspect of this 'continuous revolution' has been the constant change of senior ministers at the DFE. Since 1987, Kenneth Baker has given way to John MacGregor, MacGregor to Kenneth Clarke, and, following the 1992 General Election, Clarke to John Patten. Each of these changes has also brought about changes in other Ministerial posts within the DFE. Only during John MacGregor's tenure, ended by Margaret Thatcher in her last weeks in office, can there be said to have been any degree of constructive relationship between Ministers and education professionals. The other Ministers appear to have produced varying degrees of hostility and animosity, especially during Clarke's tenure, when he was assisted by Michael Fallon and Tim Eggar, vigorous supporters of the reforms from the Thatcherite right of the Conservative Party. Simon (1992) describes how these Ministers' actions appeared to court confrontation with teachers and local authorities.

It was also during Clarke's period in office at the DFE, in the summer of 1991, that the chairs of both the NCC and SEAC suddenly 'retired', to be replaced respectively by a former member and a former head of the Downing Street Policy Unit. Chitty (1992) suggests that these moves signify that the government at that moment dropped any pretence that the National Curriculum will be 'politically neutral'.

Clarke also oversaw the introduction of the Parent's Charter, born of the Citizen's Charter initiative, which promised parents more information about their children's education and more say in the running of schools. The Charter was given legislative form in the Education (Schools) Act 1992, which required the publication of information by schools, in order that the controversial 'league tables' could be produced, and, reformed the local inspection arrangements for schools. In the last weeks before the 1992 General Election, the government's proposals on inspection were significantly watered down in the House of Lords. In its amended form, the Act has the effect of allowing HMI a continuing role in overseeing inspection rather than allowing, as originally envisaged, schools the power to appoint their own inspectors.

The Act further concentrates power in the hands of central government. In providing for the appointment by the Secretary of State of HM Chief Inspector of Schools, the Act also states explicitly (Section 2(6)) that, 'In exercising his functions the Chief Inspector of Schools for England shall have regard to such aspects of government policy as the Secretary of State may direct'.

Following the General Election victory of 1992, a new Secretary of State for Education, John Patten, was appointed. Patten quickly acquired a high public profile; within days of his appointment it was being reported (*The Guardian*, 17 April 1992) that he was extolling the value of religious faith in 'redemption and damnation' in the fight against rising crime and more generally in defence of traditional moral values, and that schools, as surrogate parents, had a role to play in inculcating such beliefs.

The 1992 White Paper

When, only three months after his appointment, Patten had produced the White Paper, *Choice and Diversity* (DFE, 1992), it was clear that the pace of educational change was unlikely to slacken in the foreseeable future. What was equally clear from the White Paper was that the direction of change remained unaltered; both in rhetoric and substance the White Paper, and Education Bill (which only emerged from the parliamentary process as the Education Act 1993 while this book was being completed) build upon the edifice created by the ERA.

Although the themes of choice, diversity, accountability and standards remain to the fore, it is clear that the proposals also represent a direct response to some of the planning difficulties created by the ERA. By atomizing local power, and divesting the LEA of the power to plan and manage a local schools system, significant problems (discussed in Chapters 3 and 4) have already arisen and, if opting-out takes off, will be greatly exacerbated in relation to school provision and especially admissions. However, it would have been surprising had the government chosen to reinvest local government with such powers, and the mechanisms envisaged in the White Paper consist of new quangos, staffed by government appointees, without any democratically elected element.

As with the ERA, the White Paper contains internal contradictions in relation to the twin goals of dissemination of power and centralization, though the White Paper also raises directly a conflict well hidden in the ERA. As will be discussed in the next chapter, choice of school depends crucially upon the availability of capacity at desirable schools; in the absence of spare places, the potential for choice is non-existent. However, in addition to espousing parental choice as a central plank of government policy, the White Paper also stresses the need to remove surplus capacity in the school system, in the interests of economic efficiency. It is unclear which of these two apparently incompatible aims will be allowed to win out in practice.

As will be discussed in Chapter 3, it can be argued that even before the 1992 White Paper, opting-out was the lynch-pin of the whole scheme of reform. The White Paper confirms this view, with targets being set for a rapid acceleration in the rate of opting-out, though apparently with no new incentives, and perhaps even disincentives in financial terms, to opt out. In an effort to encourage more moves to GM status, the White Paper suggests that smaller primary schools, for whom opting-out has yet not seemed attractive, may wish to opt out in 'clusters'; the conflict between the supposed fundamental purpose of opting-out under the ERA, greater autonomy, and the loss of independence associated with cluster arrangements as envisaged by the White Paper, does not seem to have struck the paper's authors. At the same time, restrictions are proposed on the amounts LEAs may spend in campaigns opposing opting-out.

The new quangos will take the form of Education Associations (EAs) and a Funding Agency for Schools (FAS). The former will be established locally, though appointed by central government, and will in essence be a 'task force', sent in to take over the LEA and governing bodies' powers and oversee schools identified as 'failing', with the objective of 'turning the business round', with an ultimate aim of releasing the school into the GM sector.

The FAS, will gradually take over responsibility for management of the schools system, and the distribution of funds from LEAs as increasing numbers of schools opt out. Again, nationally appointed, it will fulfil many functions currently carried out in relation to the small GM sector by the DFE. It seems inevitable that such a body, if the GM sector grows at anything like the rate envisaged in the White Paper, will ultimately have to establish regional or local offices; rather like LEAs, but without the local democratic basis.

The White Paper proposals consist of a curious mix of prescriptions, for quangos, new powers to intervene in GM schools, and apparently pious hopes, such as the desire for schools to cooperate on admissions, and for the removal of surplus places. Contradictions, between choice and removing surplus capacity, between the supposed decentralization and practical centralization, and between stressing the institutional independence of schools and the imposition of a new tier of bureaucracy to supervise them, abound.

Indeed, even in its rhetoric the White Paper is less clear-cut than that produced by the ERA's supporters in 1987 and 1988. While there is no doubt that the White Paper is a continuation of the process set in train by the ERA and pursued in the Parent's Charter initiative, there are clearly also some changes in approach. At times, the spirit of former Prime Minister Thatcher is clearly present: 'Parents know best the needs of their children – certainly better than educational theorists or administrators, better even than our mostly excellent teachers.' However, in other places the text of the White Paper raises the possibility that, contrary to Thatcher's stated belief, there is such a thing as society, or at least community, for example when it refers to 'the community of which it [the school] forms an integral part and on which it depends', and, 'it is that community involvement which will be essential to the future success of the schools concerned'.

Opponents of the reforms should not, however, take any great comfort or hope from the presence of internal inconsistencies within the White Paper proposals. As has already been demonstrated, ERA is also riddled with conflicts and contradictions, yet this has not prevented it from altering the shape of education in England and Wales.

Given the nature of party politics at Westminster, it was always highly unlikely that the parliamentary process will reject the major thrust of the 1992 Education Bill, deriving closely from the White Paper, on such grounds. Indeed, those who observed the passage of the ERA through Parliament will have experienced a strong sense of *déjà vu* over the winter and spring of 1992–3.

The Second Reading debate on the 255 clauses of the 1992 Bill took place in early November 1992. In it Ann Taylor, Labour's education spokesperson, echoed by Don Foster for the Liberal Democrats, described the Bill as a 'dangerous irrelevancy', and a 'further reckless attack on local government'. On 15 December, with the Bill in Committee, a guillotine motion was successfully passed by the government in the face of strong opposition, effectively setting a timetable and restricting debate on the Bill. Consideration by the Commons of amendments introduced in the House of Lords was also curtailed by a guillotine on 19 July 1993. Despite a slimmer majority in the Commons than in 1987, the Conservative government seems likely again to imprint its design upon the system of schools in England and Wales.

A retreat from ERA?

In the summer of 1993, in the wake of the teachers' boycott of Key stage Three tests, Sir Ron Dearing, Chairman designate of SCAA, released a report favouring a slimmed-down national curriculum, allowing teachers more time and freedom to control the content of teaching. At the same time, proposals were brought forward to modify testing arrangements and end the publication of league tables relating to test results at age seven and fourteen (*The Observer*, 1 August 1993).

The fact that the government appeared willing to accept such proposals suggests a not insignificant retreat, and may demonstrate a greater willingness to listen to unwelcome advice rather than to react to it by changing the adviser. However, though such moves may bring the government short-term relief from teacher hostility, they scarcely amount to a reversal of the broad thrust of government policy or an abandonment of the fundamental principles underlying recent reform.

PARALLEL DEVELOPMENTS

On comparative methods

Kahn-Freund (1974), considering comparative law techniques, notes that, 'comparative method . . . requires a knowledge not only of the foreign law, but also of its social, and above all its political context'. However, if this *caveat* is borne in mind, judicious use of comparisons from other jurisdictions can often prove enlightening for lawyers, other social scientists, and students of social policy implementation such as the initiatives in education with which this book is concerned.

The kind of reforms introduced into state schooling in Britain, changing the role of state bodies in the provision of education, is by no means unique. Indeed, as Osborne and Gaebler (1992) demonstrate, similar phenomena can be observed in a number of 'Western' countries, not only in relation to schooling, but across the entire range of what have traditionally been considered 'public' services.

Though the scope of this work does not allow for the detailed exposition of comparisons between developments in educational administration in England and Wales and other jurisdictions, the following chapters refer to some parallel developments in other countries, namely, Scotland, the USA, and New Zealand, which are introduced here. As will be immediately apparent, such comparisons do not present enormous problems given the relative political and cultural similarity of these countries with England and Wales. However, differences in the legal and political systems, and, in particular the very different, federal, constitutional basis for public administration in the USA, demand circumspection, and a continuing awareness of Kahn-Freund's point, when attempting comparison.

Scotland

Though part of the UK, Scotland has a distinctive institutional history. The Treaty of Union 1707 expressly provided for the maintenance of separate foundations for certain Scottish institutions, most notably the Church, the system of common law, and, the universities. The tradition of separate legislation for education in Scotland continues to the present.

As Kahn-Freund himself indicates, 'Scotland retains her separate judicial organisations and procedures, solemnly guaranteed by the Act of Union', and Kellas (1984) identifies Scottish education as 'one of the best defined arenas of Scottish life and one that most maintains the boundaries of the Scottish political system'. The works of McPherson and Raab (1988) and Humes (1986) also point towards a rather different policy-making community in Scottish education to that south of the border.

Comparison between Scotland and England and Wales is particularly attractive in education, where broadly similar trends have taken different legislative form, and have formed part of a distinctive political agenda. Unlike the single major upheaval created south of the border by ERA in 1988, parental choice had been given a strong form in 1981 (Adler *et al.*, 1989), while the equivalent of governing bodies, bodies with a long history in England and Wales, school boards, were only brought about under the School Boards Act 1988, and, opting-out was introduced in Scotland one year later by the Self-Governing Schools, etc. (Scotland) Act 1989. School boards in Scotland, somewhat curiously, unlike their counterparts in England and Wales, carry a parental majority, although they have been granted fewer powers than exist under the ERA, and have shown a marked reluctance to seek to extend the powers available to them (Munn 1991).

This piecemeal development in Scotland reflects a degree of continuity in the administration of education in Scotland, contrasting with the upheavals created in 1988 south of the border. This relative continuity seems to go some of the way to explaining the total lack of interest in opting out in Scotland, referred to in Chapter 3.

United States of America

Within the federal system of the USA, education is primarily a state matter, and in practice delegated to some 16,000 'local education agencies' (LEAgs) (Sky, 1989). However, as Sky (1992) indicates, local educational developments remain susceptible to influence by the agenda of the national government, and indeed President Bush's Republican administration spent large sums on the development of local programmes to enhance parental choice of school (Hodges, 1991).

Coons (1986) paints a picture in which only modest moves towards parental choice can be discerned. However, with the active support of Bush's administration, initiatives introduced at both state and local agency level since then have pursued, *inter alia*,

- increased parental participation (including enhanced choice of school)
- delegation of responsibilities to schools
- enhanced recognition and incentives for teachers

While the first two of these ends may seem very familiar to observers of British education, the last may well come as something of a surprise, reflecting perhaps the narrow basis of recent British reforms.

It is interesting to observe that trends towards enhanced parental choice including programmes to facilitate both intra- and inter-district mobility, invariably retain active, structural and informing, roles remaining for LEAgs (e.g. Cambridge, Massachusetts), and, are limited in such a way as to ensure that the measures do not clash with broader initiatives in social policy such as desegregation plans (e.g. Minnesota). Other schemes, such as that in Wisconsin, have begun to include funding for children from low-income families, who are performing poorly in state schools, to attend private schools. Sky (1992) notes the critical importance of adequate information and the provision of transport if parental choice is to be more than tokenistic.

Meanwhile 'Charter Schools' are being established in areas including California and Minnesota, in response to the demands of specific groups of parents. Such schools may be based on or within existing schools, or can, if adequate sponsorship can be found, be built from scratch, though in the California scheme adequate support from teachers is required. Observing a fascinating parallel to opting-out in Britain, Parker (1993) notes that some schools have sought Charter status solely to avoid closure.

At the same time, in a similar development, 'magnet' schools have been developed in School District 4, East Harlem, one of the most socially deprived areas of New York City. Smaller than typical district schools, and able to specialize, in an effort to attract different constituencies of parents, such schools appear to offer greater diversity than existed before. Again though, the education-specific developments are subject to the more general requirements of a social programme relating to racial balance (Garnett, 1993).

The system of public education system, currently being 'reinvented', in the USA, has been summarized thus:

State governments and school boards would steer the system but let others row. They would set minimum standards, measure performance, enforce goals such as racial integration and social equity, and establish the financing mechanisms necessary to achieve their standards and goals. Public schools would be run – on something like a contract or voucher basis – by many different organizations: teachers, colleges, even community organizations. It would be relatively easy to create a new public school. Teachers would work for the school, not the school district. Steering would be separate from rowing.

(Osborne and Gaebler, 1992, p. 316)

As in Britain, choice and improved outcomes in terms of educational standards are key agenda items. However, important differences emerge in the clear identification of overriding, equity based, social policy goals in the US context, and, the central role given to teachers in the new structures, unlike their British counterparts.

Parker (1993) suggests that another important difference is that the diverse developments in the USA have taken place within a spirit of experimentation, rather than what he characterizes as a policy of 'legislate first and ask questions after' in Britain.

New Zealand

With a population of less than 4 million, the education system in New Zealand operates on a radically different scale to that of the USA, or even England and Wales. However, developments in the late 1980s, initially under the Labour government of David Lange, provide a further example of parallel developments in the administration of state schooling.

New Zealand has a strong tradition of centralized control of the curriculum, dating back, states Codd (1981), to the Education Act of 1877 which vested responsibility for the curriculum in the Department of Education. More recently, in 1942, the Thomas Report established a set of 'core' requirements (Codd, 1991). However, it is suggested that this fact has not prevented a diversity in schools in terms of principles and teaching methods especially since the introduction of new measures following the investigations of a 'task force' established by Lange in 1987 which resulted in the Picot Report of 1988.

Beckett (1991) points towards three significant developments under the initiative in the late 1980s. First, she refers to a provision, apparently akin to Charter Schools in the USA, which allows the parents of a minimum of 21 children at a school to break away and establish a new school if they wish to do so; she refers to the provision being used mostly by groups wishing to establish Maori language schools, but also cites an example of a Steiner school now receiving state funding under this scheme.

Secondly, she points towards the establishment of 'Community Education

Forums', in which an official from the Department of Education will spend a term working with the schools and community of a locality in order to facilitate the debate on educational change.

Thirdly, she refers to responsibility for school management having been transferred from the Department of Education to a board of trustees in each school, which has an in-built parent majority. Each board of trustees prepares a document, or 'charter', described by Beckett as 'a contract between the community, the school and the state', which is subject to Ministerial approval. This legal document is viewed by Codd (1991) as 'the lynchpin of the whole Picot structure', though he remains unclear as to exactly what the consequences of such institutional charters will be.

Beckett notes that the replacement of Labour with a National Party government in October 1990 may leave these reforms looking rather like 'hostages to fortune'. She suggests that although decisions had not then been taken in relation to fundamental changes in policy, in her words 'ominously Thatcherite' tendencies can now be seen in official rhetoric on education, suggesting that the reforms have not gone far enough. While under the Labour government, ministerial approval for school charters would not be granted unless they contained a clause relating to striving for equality, the National Party Education Minister has indicated that this will no longer be required. She notes also that the new government wants to move to increase parental choice, and has hinted at a system of education vouchers.

However, a familiar conflict between choice and cost-efficiency may have to be faced by the National government. The measures introduced by Labour are clearly expensive, especially in their tendency to produce small schools. Though seeking to enhance choice, the government may have to face a similar conflict as that raised by the 1992 White Paper for England and Wales in relation to enhanced choice and elimination of surplus capacity.

It seems that the debate regarding linkage of reform to educational standards has also proceeded in a familiar vein. Parker-Jenkins (1992) describes how in New Zealand, as in Britain, 'Both governments espouse rhetoric on the concept of equal opportunities for all children, yet seek to compare schools as units of analysis in the crudest of terms.'

New Zealand provides an interesting example of parallel change in education administration having been introduced by a government of a very different complexion to those that have promoted change in Britain or USA. Beckett believes that, 'New Zealand's version of LMS gave parents a great deal more power than the British version, and arrived without any of the ideological baggage.'

However, Codd (1991) helpfully identifies the reforms in New Zealand as a consequence of a 'policy coup' in the mid-1980s, 'in which monetarist solutions were presented as the only viable responses to the immense economic problems faced by the new Labour government'. It appears therefore that although the particular form of solutions recently adopted to address perceived problems of education administration are generally connected with the programmes of right-wing administrations they do not necessarily derive from a specific set of political beliefs. Rather, they appear contingent upon the adoption of a particular response to macroeconomic problems.

The hegemony of monetarist policies, and the connected concept of the state as developed under Thatcherism and Reaganism, ultimately appears to provide the underlying common basis for the recent reforms of education in Britain, the USA and New Zealand.

WHAT HAS PUBLIC LAW GOT TO DO WITH IT?

It would not be surprising if many readers, including some lawyers, were to ask at this stage 'What has public law got to do with all this?', or indeed, the broader question of 'What is public law?' The questions arise out of a perception that most of what has gone before, and much of what is to come in this book, is likely to be viewed as what might be categorized as 'political' rather than 'legal' issues.

This categorization is quite understandable, given the dominant tradition in British legal scholarship of viewing and presenting the law in a narrow way, manifested typically in the chronicling or cataloguing of law via detailed scrutiny of cases and statutory material. While there is undoubtedly a role for such a process, the task achieves little in terms of understanding the relationship between law and other social phenomena. A single cell, examined under a microscope, in isolation from its surrounding cells, tells only a limited amount about the functioning and purposes of the organ or body of which it forms an integral part. No matter how strong the magnification, little sense of the role or purpose of the wider body will be revealed by such scrutiny, indeed as magnification increases and focus narrows, it is possible that although more minute detail may become visible, even less will be revealed about the relationship of the cell in question to its surroundings. It is thus with the kind of fastidious examination and description of legal rules that typifies so much of traditional legal scholarship; though it may be possible via such examination to describe every subtle difference between competing interpretations of a statute, such a process will tell us little about the statute's purpose or effects outside of the courtroom. Such traditional, 'black letter', study of legal doctrine fails to observe law in its social and political context, and indeed will fail to consider at all much of what can be described as 'the living law' (Ehrlich, 1922) discussed in Chapter 4.

Among other purposes of this book, one is to consider the actual and potential roles of law in education administration. What follows in the remainder of this chapter is not an attempt to pre-empt discussion that will take place in the rest of this book, but is rather an attempt to clarify the author's perspective, and to highlight some major themes that will be returned to.

The study of Public Law as an academic discipline in British universities covers much that was traditionally taught as, often separate, courses in 'constitutional' and 'administrative' law. Such courses often fell within the narrow, doctrinal approach outlined above, frequently as a result of the failure to challenge the peculiarly persistent and influential, if anachronistic, view of the constitution espoused by Dicey in the late nineteenth century.

Much of what this book considers could be reduced, from a 'traditional' lawyer's point of view, to a consideration of the legal rules that govern such issues as how the National Curriculum will be drawn up, how the governing body of a GM school will be constituted, how parents may exercise their right to state a preference for a school for their child, and, in each case, how the law will resolve disputes if it is alleged that a public body has failed to exercise its duty, or has exceeded its powers in respect of one of these issues. This would focus on the technical aspects of the core of administrative law, the domain of judicial review, and, at best, would go beyond mere description to ask questions such as whether concepts such as 'vires' and 'reasonableness' are adequate, or perhaps inquiring into the appropriateness of adversarial techniques for the resolution of complex policy issues. Some of these matters are considered in Chapter 4.

However, this book has as a central concern a focus derived from the other major aspect of public law, that is constitutionality. Though Britain, unlike the United States, has no written constitution, a constitution does exist in the sense that a series of rules, and perhaps more commonly conventions and norms, exist that intend to establish the limits of legitimate institutional power. However, this observation remains essentially descriptive, and fails to enlighten as to the purpose of the constitution.

Lewis (1993a) has written that 'A central pillar of the British constitution . . . relates to legitimate processes for decision making. What this in effect amounts to is the demand for rational discourse at the institutional level.' In this sense, the institutional arrangements for the distribution of a public good, or scarce resource, such as education, or health care (see Longley, 1993), amount to a constitutional issue, and thus one of major significance to the public lawyer.

A number of other issues that will be developed later should now be pointed towards. They all demonstrate the importance of the public law perspective on the issues discussed in this book. In the exercise of public power, 'legitimacy' is heavily dependent upon 'accountability'; both concepts to be explored further in the next chapter. One aspect of accountability in this sense is susceptibility to legal challenge. Thus, a decision maker will be answerable in court if their decision is found to have been taken outside their powers, or without adherence to legally required procedures. Such a process is clearly relevant to all levels of decision making in the administration of public education, from the Secretary of State to the governing body of a GM school. Indeed, as Milman (1986) and others have noted, the courts have been looked to increasingly in recent times to determine disputes regarding educational administration. Though often superficially based around narrow legal points, such disputes as that arising out of the approval of GM status for Beechen Cliff School in Avon, discussed in Chapters 3 and 4, also raise more fundamental issues regarding the location of decision-making power and constitutionality.

Similarly, commentators note a general tendency towards the increased use of law as an instrument of policy implementation by central government. Thus, whereas in the past persuasion and informal direction might have been used to bring about reform, in recent times, as 'consensus' in education administration has turned into 'conflict', central government has tended to use primary legislation and statutory instruments in such a way as to force LEAs to implement policies they might otherwise have rejected. Such a tendency can be viewed as one example of a broader trend in central/local government relations that has, under recent Conservative administrations, resulted in local authorities becoming increasingly rule-bound agencies (Loughlin, 1989).

The process of juridification, encompassing both increased litigation and legal instrumentalism, locates decision making in educational administration clearly within the domain of the public lawyer.

Almost thirty years ago Mitchell (1965), noting the common law roots of British public law, wrote of the contrast between the rapid growth and evolution of private law in the nineteenth century and 'the failure of lawyers to produce a similar evolution in the field of public law even when the needs for such an evolution have become apparent'. He quotes Lord Devlin as observing, eight years earlier, that 'The common law has now, I think, no longer the strength to provide any satisfactory solution to the problem of keeping the executive, with all the powers which under modern conditions are needed for the efficient conduct of the realm, under proper control.' More recently, Prosser (1982) has noted again the failure to develop an autonomous public law system in Britain, a problem he believes derives at least in part from what he views as 'the absence of a tradition of the state as a theoretical and political concept in England'.

From this broad public law perspective, perhaps the single most important aspect of the complex policy-making process is its frequent inexplicitness. The legislative framework is such that there is little requirement for systematic or open policy making, and as a result, the potential exists for policy to develop in a piecemeal and haphazard manner, influenced more by the fluctuating, uncertain and essentially hidden relationship between central and local administrators than by any clearly articulated and definable system or principles.

In terms of the agenda set out above, a crucial role for the public lawyer is that of institutional design in decision-making processes. Within the broad remit of ensuring that institutional arrangements meet the essential constitutional purpose, that an arena for rational discourse is established and maintained, public lawyers must address the specific issues of whether appropriate and effective institutional mechanisms for accountability exist, and whether, with the increasing use of litigation, to resolve complex policy/resource allocation issues, a legal framework can be established to facilitate rational decision making in this forum.

Thus a public lawyer may enter into a 'political' arena such as the administration of education without apology. It is clear that law is inextricably implicated in such an area of public life. Indeed, in many ways the law can assume the character of what Stewart (1975) has referred to as a 'surrogate political process'. In taking on such a task, however, the public lawyer is seeking not to replace political processes with legal mechanisms, but rather, seeking to ensure the fundamental constitutional purpose of maximization of rational discourse in public policy-making. As Harden and Lewis (1986) have expressed it, such an approach is not an attempt 'to replace politics by law but to harness legal institutions to explore and facilitate policy making and create the optimum conditions for political choice'.

This first chapter has sought to set the recent reforms of education in their context, demonstrating the overlap between social, political and legal issues in this area. It has described how emphases have shifted, and how the law has been heavily implicated in such changes, and, has suggested a central role for public lawyers in ensuring conformity with constitutional expectations in the delivery of state education. These themes are returned to throughout this book, and in the next chapter a more detailed exploration is undertaken of the linkage between the central concepts of accountability, choice and standards in schooling.

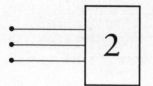

2

CONCEPTS AND CONNECTIONS: SCHOOLING AND CITIZENSHIP

INDIVIDUAL AND COLLECTIVE GOALS, AND EDUCATIONAL STANDARDS

As was noted in Chapter 1, the broad objectives of schooling in the post-war era were indicated in the White Paper, *Educational Reconstruction* (DFE, 1943):

> to secure for children a happier childhood and a better start in life; to ensure a fuller measure of education and opportunity for young people and to provide means for all of developing the various talents with which they are endowed and so enriching the inheritance of the country whose citizens they are.

Though it would be naïve to treat such a quotation as a comprehensive statement of the purposes of an entire school system, it does represent a convenient starting point for any exploration of the educational enterprise. Its weakness is perhaps that it does not explicitly state the egalitarian spirit that most commentators find embodied in the 1944 Act.

The quotation does, however, raise issues that will be of central concern throughout this chapter, as it refers to children as 'citizens', indicating that the education process is intended not only to offer them opportunities as individuals, but also as members of a collective group. If the purpose of schooling is thus viewed as twofold, to offer benefits to individuals and to society as a whole, the potential tensions between competing claims, referred to by Finch (1984) are again brought to the fore. This tension will be a recurrent theme in this chapter.

This book does not, however, concern itself with the delivery of such educational aims, in the sense of classroom practice, but rather with the mechanisms that are employed, at a national, local and individual school level for enabling or facilitating the delivery of education in pursuit of the aims identified. It is with the decision-making processes inherent in educational administration that I am concerned, though for such a discussion to take place without any concept of educational aims might be considered somewhat foolish; there is little point inquiring as to the efficiency of a rail service in meeting its timetable without having some idea as to whether the trains run to places people want to go.

Recent discussions of the reform of education have been remarkably weak in this respect. While 'standards' has been a familiar term in the educational debate for some 20 years or more, it has remained by and large, outside specialist circles, an undeveloped and nebulous concept. The claims of those who introduced market forces into education in the ERA and the subsequent reforms have consistently been that the intention was to enhance educational standards. However, it has proven difficult to assess the actual impact of the reforms. Such evidence as has emerged so far has done little to indicate any success for the reforms in this respect (Ofsted, 1993), though it is early days, and cannot be taken as a definitive outcome, especially given the inadequacy of the conceptual development relating to standards.

Evaluation of school effectiveness, as demonstrated in the work of Riddell and Brown (1991), discussed below, emerges as a complex and difficult subject which does not lend itself to analysis via simple comparisons or league tables. Such a subject requires expertise which the present author neither possesses nor claims, but it is important that the existence of such complexities, at the heart of the education debate, is indicated at the outset. It is a theme to which we will return.

However, this book is centred on the administration of education, rather than educational outcomes *per se*, though inevitably, as one is the means to the other, the two cannot be neatly separated. Clearly, the objectives of the institutional arrangements of administration, should be measured, and acquire legitimacy, to some extent by reference to the outcomes of the process. However, it is equally clear that legitimacy in educational administration derives from more than simply the attainment or failure to attain stated objectives.

Ranson and Stewart (1989), in considering the role of management in the public sector highlight the fundamental relationship between collective choice and the public domain. They consider that the essence of political discourse regarding the distribution of a public good such as education is the exercise of collective choice. They note that 'citizenship', being part of the political community, implies both rights and active participation, and consider that a necessary condition for the continuation of a public domain is the achievement of a balance between participation and representative government, plus, public accountability. In this sense, a critical function of management in the public domain is the production, preservation and facilitation of all aspects of this equation.

This can be said to be a reformulation of the point made by Lewis (1993a), referred to in Chapter 1, above. In the specific context of distribution of a public good, such as education, Lewis has also noted that

> equality of citizenship counts too; to put it another way, equity is often a core concern in the delivery of public services in a way that is often inappropriate in the private sector. Where there is no real market for public services – where there is no real opportunity to shop around – then equity among citizens is paramount, just as there may well be need to ration and therefore to set priorities according to publicly agreed agenda.
>
> (Lewis, 1993b, p. 21)

Taken as a whole, Lewis's work suggests that the process of rational discourse remains the essential justificatory basis for public sector management and intervention, whether the dominant decision-making structure is that of a 'social market' or otherwise. Thus, the process demands at least as much attention as the outcomes.

LEGITIMACY

The legitimacy of government therefore derives not only from the attainment or failure to attain objectives, but also from the mechanisms used to achieve such ends.

Traditionally in Britain, executive action, in education and most policy fields, has been legitimated by reference to one or more of three claims. Frequently, reference is made to the legal basis for powers; that they have been conferred by statute, or by common law, and that their exercise is subject to review by the courts. Secondly, government will often refer to the role of Parliament in overseeing executive action, of accountability to the electorate 'through the ballot box', and the adherence to politico-administrative conventions. Additionally, as already noted, the achievement of economic growth has traditionally been cited as establishing the legitimacy of government action (Graham and Prosser, 1988).

In the interest of clarity, it is worth emphasizing that this book is informed by a belief that legitimacy in the exercise of political power derives from more than 'lawfulness' alone. Evidence of the wide acceptance of this is abundant, in that the adherence or non-adherence to conventions, not legally enforceable, is a major factor in the claims of legitimacy put forward by power holders in Britain.

Ultimately, it appears that it is the potential for being called to account, legally, parliamentarily, electorally, or through other extra-parliamentary activity, which underlies claims of legitimacy for British government. Though the range of such devices is wide, it would be complacent to believe that the mechanisms for accountability which exist are necessarily adequate to justify the claims of legitimacy laid upon them by those who govern. In light of the crucial importance of accountability mechanisms, it is necessary to subject them to careful and critical evaluation.

ACCOUNTABILITY

Ranson and Stewart (1989, p. 18) note that when decisions have been made regarding an issue of public choice such as education policy,

> those in public office have to be held to account for the authority they have exercised on behalf of the public. Power is legitimated in our democracy by the consent of the public who have granted authority to elected representatives and officials on the condition that they are to account to the public for their actions.

Accountability in this context can be considered as the processes whereby those that exercise power are subjected to effective scrutiny, and if necessary effective challenge and sanction, in order to seek to ensure that the exercise of power is within prescribed limits, and within the terms of a conception of the public will. While the primary purpose of such processes will be to ensure legitimacy, it is often the case that one of the criteria applied will be some conception of 'efficiency'. In this sense, a secondary role of accountability mechanisms can be said to be as a check on 'efficiency' in relation to substantive standards.

Kogan (1988), seeking to establish the patterns of accountability in public sector education in Britain prior to ERA, sets out three ideal typical models that have been employed. First, he refers to the, predominant, traditional public political model, based around familiar political and legal checks and balances, including aspects of democratic control. Secondly, he identifies mechanisms for accountability via professional controls, including peer group report and evaluation. Finally, he points towards consumerist models of accountability, based either on partnership between education professionals and lay service-users, and active 'consumer' participation, or, on quasi-market principles (Glennerster, 1991; Le Grand, 1991).

When considering the ERA, it is important to remember the great stress placed upon enhanced accountability in educational decision-making by the Act's framers and defenders. This accountability was largely to take the form of increased availability of choice to individual 'consumers'. 'Consumers', in the context of the ERA as it applies to primary and secondary education, were primarily defined as parents of schoolchildren, though, in the increased role for local business on school governing bodies and TECs, an additional constituency of consumers appears to have been identified.

Clearly, this form of accountability, a subsection of the Kogan's third category, derives from a very different base to those emanating from the legal principles, or, principles of administrative practice referred to above. Instead, accountability, and hence legitimacy, is said to derive from the exercise of a quasi-market, which claims to empower service users through the provision of limited choice for individuals. Decision-making power was to be taken from the 'educational establishment' and placed in the hands of 'consumers'.

As stated above, accountability in public arenas in Britain has generally been seen to derive from one or more of three sources: the representative basis of democratically elected government (central and local) and 'checks and balances' within the system, the potential for judicial review of official action (in relation to the exercise of delegated powers), and, most recently, the exercise of market principles.

Table 2.1 illustrates in a simplified form the manner in which, in the course of a stated attempt to improve educational standards, not only is accountability seen to have changed its form, with market forces replacing local democratic processes as the primary mechanism of accountability relevant to the administration of education, but the same mechanism of market forces has become the principle accountability mechanism and the crucial element in the decision-making process – and one in which community goals no longer have an informing presence.

Table 2.1   Differences in the principal mechanisms of decision making, accountability, and, educational aims, before and after the ERA

	Pre-ERA	*Post-ERA*
Decisions	via local democratic processes	via market forces
Accountability	via democratic processes via law	via market forces via law
Educational aims	school effectiveness and efficiency concern with individual child equity and community goals	school effectiveness and efficiency concern with individual child

I will now briefly consider the impact of the ERA on accountability deriving from each of these three sources, political processes, legal redress, and market forces.

Accountability via political processes

The ERA reforms of education must be viewed in the context of a general realignment of power between central and local government brought about during the Thatcher period. Loughlin (1989) identifies as part of that reform a process of juridification, both as an end in itself, in order to render local authorities more rule-bound, but also as a necessity in order to fill the normative gap resulting from tensions and breakdowns in the pre-existing networks and relationships between central and local government.

The ERA reforms appear to have resulted in a significant centralization of substantive power, while simultaneously undermining the power of LEAs to plan and manage a local system of schools. That the end of this process has not yet been reached is evident from a glance at the 1992 White Paper, and from recent proposals from the Centre for Policy Studies (Lister, 1991).

In the exercise of such powers as the approval of GM schools, drawing up regulations on the National Curriculum and testing arrangements, and approving LMS schemes and devising regulations for the scheme's overall administration, the power of the Secretary of State is fettered only by his responsibility to Parliament, a mechanism of doubtful effectiveness in the modern era, argue Harden and Lewis (1986), and, notionally, by the Courts, though as the litigation discussed at Chapters 3 and 4, below, illustrates, the Secretary of State's discretion remains wide.

The appointment and replacement of Chairs and other members of the National Curriculum Council and SEAC, referred to in Chapter 1, illustrates the range of power available to the Secretary of State.

Bogdanor (1991), discussing accountability in education after the ERA, states that, 'we have not yet found a method, within the confines of ministerial responsibility, of making centralised public services properly accountable'. By way of contrast, he appears to see some hope of greater accountability in local democratic processes, noting that, 'Local authorities, at their best, make possible a process of public dialogue which is part of the very purpose of representative institutions.' He seems to suggest, like Partington and Wragg (1989), Ranson (1990a) and Sallis (1988) *inter alia*, that participative mechanisms and representative institutions are not necessarily mutually exclusive.

On a similar theme, Gann (1991) notes the impact of formula funding on community use of school sites, reporting that financial pressures on some schools are resulting in them charging for the use of school facilities at rates that effectively exclude certain local groups. Combined with the effect of the potential for opting-out as a disincentive for local authorities to embark on dual school/community use projects, even LEA maintained schools appear to be further removed from the wider community in which they are located. For GM schools, the potential is obviously still greater.

In seeking to project some hope for the future of local authorities, Bogdanor (1991) points towards the concept of 'subsidiarity' in the law of the European Communities. He believes, however, that 'It will be a sad reflection on our system if we have to look to the Community to rejuvenate our democratic traditions because we are unable to do it for ourselves.'

Accountability via redress mechanisms

Drawing extensively on the work of Lewis *et al.* (1987), the National Consumer Council report, *When Things Go Wrong At School* (1992) focuses on redress procedures in the education service. Though identifying a range of formal, statutory mechanisms for redress, on matters as diverse as complaints regarding religious worship, delivery of the National Curriculum, admissions and exclusions appeals, and, special educational needs, the report notes that this collection of procedures 'scarcely adds up to a redress system – partly because of its haphazardness, but mainly because it does not cover the whole range of educational problems'. To this collection of avenues for redress should be added, in limited circumstances, others such as complaints to the Commissioner for Local Administration (CLA), judicial review, and a range of non-statutory local complaints procedures.

Despite the panoply of redress mechanisms, the National Consumer Council report states clearly that, 'the vast majority of grievances are handled at school level'. It notes also that schools have substantial freedom in how they deal with parental complaints, 'mostly unhampered by external supervision', and that this remains an area in which there is substantial delegation of responsibilities from governing bodies to headteachers. The report identifies a problem in assessing the effectiveness of internal complaints procedures both at school and LEA level, brought about by a dearth of recorded data.

The report appears to reveal redress procedures in public education as a congeries of inconsistent and *ad hoc* responses, within which wide variations in effectiveness and accessibility exist. It concludes that, 'The government has made shifting the balance of power between parents and professionals a policy goal, but there is no convincing evidence that it has a coherent view of how redress mechanisms fit into its strategy.'

Accountability via market mechanisms

The National Consumer Council report identifies a clear stress by government on mechanisms for choice, information and participation, rather than on complaints and redress procedures. As has already been indicated, the Parent's Charter, and the resulting Education (Schools) Act 1992 state an intention to offer parents more information on which they can base their preferences of schools. Though there have recently been signs of a move away from this being in the form of league tables of 'raw' test results in favour of more considered, 'value added' assessments, there is likely to be continuing debate as to the worth of such information.

Brighouse and Tomlinson (1991), in considering performance indicators for 'successful' schools, expressly make the point that such measures *could* be used in the quest for successful schools for *all* children, as opposed to furthering market principles, which they state 'require, as do most markets, "winners and losers" '. However, it seems inconceivable in the foreseeable future for the government to withdraw from its basic policy of a market in education driven by parental choice and formula funding, a model which seems to derive essentially from a system based upon the differences between 'good' and 'bad' schools.

Great emphasis is placed by the government and its supporters on the active role parents can and should play in their children's education, specifically in the Parent's Charter (DFE, 1991). However, it has recently been reported in DFE funded research carried out by Hinds Education (consultants) and Birmingham University's School of Education that such involvement actually appears slight in many schools, with Annual Meetings quorate in only about 20 per cent of schools (*The Guardian*, 20 October 1992). Ultimately, it appears that substantial doubts exist as to the reality, as opposed to the rhetoric of 'consumer empowerment' in education.

One of the few certainties, though, appears to be that such market forces as do exist are producing outcomes that the government feels need to be urgently addressed. The creation of a Funding Agency and Education Associations introduced in the 1993 Act appears to confirm Bogdanor's observation that such a market requires constant regulation.

Ranson (1990a, p. 122) states that,

> If choice is to be public choice it requires there to be the opportunity for citizens to make their views known so that the inescapably diverse constituencies of education are enabled to present, discuss and negotiate their account. Public choice presupposes public participation and mutual accountability.

The point is emphasized again by Ranson and Stewart (1989), when they state that, 'The constitutive conditions for active citizenship and public choice in government are a necessary balance in the institutions of participatory and representative government.' A similar issue is taken up by Lewis (1993b) when he notes that 'The notion of a citizen captures the necessary duality as individual and as member of the community.'

The British courts have taken some steps towards enforcing participative mechanisms. In the area of representative democracy, authoritative decision making by representatives, especially in local authorities, has been in places significantly tempered by statutory requirements of consultation. Judges and tribunals (e.g. *R v South Glamorgan Appeals Committee*, ex parte *Evans*, 1984, unreported, see 1985 JSWL 162) have gone some way towards enforcing such requirements (e.g. *Lee v DES* (1967) 66 LGR 211, *Bradbury v Enfield* [1967] 1 WLR 1311), and, through the doctrine of legitimate expectation (e.g. *R v Brent LBC* ex parte *Gunning* (1985) 84 LGR 168), have arguably even created new duties of consultation. However, such judicial intervention has been sporadic and unpredictable.

The absence of systematic and comprehensive participative mechanism in education decision making does not derive from the non-availability of such devices. Indeed, there are a variety of devices by which parents could be empowered in the sphere of education.

Partington and Wragg (1989) set out a range of mechanisms by which parental influence in schools could be enhanced. Choice of school is clearly one, as is being a governor, however, they point out that parents can also become more involved and influential through a number of forms of contact with teaching staff. In addition to the common social and fund-raising parent-teacher activities, Partington and Wragg consider the potential for curriculum evenings, and encouraging parents to visit classroom to increase their understanding and involvement in current education practice. They also discuss the potential for increasing the role of parents in assisting with their children's learning, in conjunction with the provision of appropriate advice and guidance by teachers to parents.

It is clearly also possible that parents can play a useful 'quality assurance', or monitoring, role, if they are provided with suitable procedures, and adequate information on which to base feedback. 'Community schools' are also a mechanism for greater parental participation in the educational endeavour of schools, as part of wider community involvement. A further alternative is the use of home-schools contracts, allowing parents an active and central role in their children's education (see, e.g. Ross and Tomlinson, 1991).

Yet another alternative is raised by Templeton (1989), who, discusses the establishment of a Home School Council (HSC) in a Lewisham secondary school. She notes that, typically, 'Most parents do not feel they have a role to fulfil *vis-à-vis* the school; they have no obvious reason for being there at all and feel they have nothing to contribute', and, 'Apart from the small amount of information gleaned through their children, parents are left with their own experience of school as their sole guide to the institution.'

She notes also that traditional parent–teacher associations (PTAs) have generally been poor at involving parents in educational, as opposed to social or fund-raising issues. She perceives a need for a change in the relationship, a greater sense of partnership and equality, between teaching staff and parents, and a recognition of the potential contribution that each can offer, though Raab (1993), addressing the current major conceptual themes in debates on education administration, notes that 'partnership' does not necessarily imply 'equality' of input or influence.

Templeton also suggests that the post-ERA settlement may not be to the advantage of those parents whose voice is limited, and perceives a risk that even HSCs may still exclude many parents, with most active participants being of a similar social status as the teachers. These themes are returned to later in this chapter in the context of the contributions of, *inter alia*, Adler (1993) and Sams (1991).

Templeton indicates that a problem has been to establish HSCs, or other participative mechanisms, that can address and reflect the diverse needs of pupils. In a sense she seems to be echoing Warnock's views (1988) that the task in hand is to avoid 'educational waste', and to avoid the 'left-over' schools remaining after preferences have been exercised.

Warnock expresses distinct caution over parent power in education, at least in the form of 'consumerism' which she rejects as a false analogy. She suggests that parents are likely to have a short-sighted and romanticized view of schools. Their short-term interests will potentially result in lack of continuity and failure to address collective aims, and, their lack of knowledge of current educational practice, as referred to by Templeton above, leaves them largely out of touch.

However, despite the many and various alternative mechanisms of increasing parental influence in schools, the 1980 Act (and its parallel 1981 Act in Scotland), and indeed the ERA and proposals for voucher schemes, all focus almost exclusively on the provision of choice to individual parents, regarding the school their children attend, as the key mechanism of empowerment. In some ways, this narrow focus is reinforced by the work of the wider 'consumer movement', as epitomized in the National Consumer Council (1992) report into complaints procedures at schools referred to above.

Evidence from the 1980s and since the ERA tends to suggest that the net effect of this single-track model of parental empowerment is to polarize the issues of choice and planning. Effective parental choice, if widely exercised, seems likely to be incompatible with effective planning of a local system of schools.

CHOICE

Whatever happened to the voucher?

In 1986, in a publication of the Institute of Economic Affairs, Seldon (1986, p. 97) asked,

What happened to the voucher? The solution to the riddle is not administrative impracticability but official feet-dragging and political underestimation of potential popular acclaim (and its 'harvest' of votes).

Chitty (1989) notes how the concept of a voucher, provided by the state to parents, and enabling them to purchase education up to a set value either at state schools or private schools, an idea that can be traced back to Friedman in the mid-1950s, was picked up by Rhodes Boyson in the mid-1970s. Maynard (1975) identifies at least eight different potential models of voucher scheme, and concludes that experimentation is necessary. Interest in the idea derived largely from experiments in California (Coons and Sugarman, 1978), and was pursued in Britain despite strong evidence from a feasibility study carried out by Kent County Council (1978) that suggested that such a scheme would not be economically viable.

As Chitty (1989) noted, Sir Keith Joseph's attraction to the idea of education vouchers had waned by the time of the 1983 general election, apparently as a result of civil service influence. Despite this withdrawal by central government, pressure for the introduction of such a scheme continued to come from various right-wing pressure groups and 'think tanks', and the publications of the Institute for Economic Affairs, Hillgate Group and Centre for Policy Studies in the mid and late 1980s all supported the market principles underlying voucher schemes.

As can be seen, the education voucher now has a history of periodic return to prominence, and there is little doubt that some form of voucher remains the objective of certain educationists, including the influential Stuart Sexton. However, Chitty (1989) suggests that, in reality, the ERA has already brought about the incorporation of the voucher into public education, 'under a different name', in the form of open enrolment and LMS. Undoubtedly, these measures, in emphasizing the element of 'consumer' choice, supposedly now available to parents, embody many of the characteristics of voucher schemes.

The market in education

The element of choice is central to the ERA reforms. It is presented as a panacea, to solve perceived problems of inefficiency, both in terms of use of resources and in terms of educational standards. The nature of the market forces introduced into the world of schooling is often considered to represent a 'quasi-market', as although competition is introduced, the market differs from classical free markets both in respect of supply and demand sides.

Le Grand (1991) notes that, in relation to the supply side, players in markets in social policy fields such as education or health care will not necessarily be privately owned, and will not necessarily have profit maximization as their main motive. On the demand side, the 'purchaser' will not necessarily be the consumer, but will be a proxy, acting on behalf of the ultimate service user, for example a parent acting for their child, or, in health care, a general practitioner (GP) or health authority exercising the power of purchaser on behalf of patients.

It is clear that the introduction of competition between 'suppliers' (i.e. schools) fostered by the exercise of choice by 'consumers' (i.e. in the context of the ERA, parents) does indeed introduce quasi-market forces into education. In some respects the effects of such forces can be closely compared with the impact of competition between suppliers of goods (e.g. supermarkets), in that the net effect of consumer choice is likely to be that some suppliers flourish, while others fail and ultimately cease trading. Another aspect that seems remarkably similar is the additional power offered to those consumers who are sufficiently financially advantaged to be able to select from a wider range of outlets – if the quality is poor at Woolworth's, they can always try Harrods.

However, it is clear that the market in public education also differs from the supermarket situation in at least two important respects. First, it seems that children realistically have only one chance at receiving basic education; if the wrong choice is made, the option does not exist to buy a different brand, from a different shop, next time. Secondly, as Ranson (1990a) notes, market forces can actually change certain goods. As he states, 'Choice implies surplus places, but if market forces fill some schools and close others then choice evaporates leaving only a hierarchy of esteem with little actual choice for many'. He notes also that, through the exercise of choice 'the goods' may be changed at the level of individual schools:

[M]y preference for a school, privately expressed, together with the unwitting choices of others, will transform the product. A small school grows in scale with inevitable consequences for the learning style and administrative process. The distinctive ethos which was the reason for the choice may be altered by the choice.

(Ranson, 1990b, p. 14)

Ranson is identifying the same phenomenon as David Miliband (1991) does when he discusses 'interdependent decisions'. Miliband states that market choices, such as those exercised by parents in choosing a school 'are necessarily made at the margin, according to a snapshot of the incentives facing each individual'. He identifies the potential for what he terms a 'tipping effect', where a few such decisions may lead to more following suit, and an unstoppable momentum being created. Such drastic swings, either to or from an individual school, will inevitably result in the school, and therefore its 'educational product', changing. He also points towards the specific potential, at a local level, for the exercise of such choice leading to racial segregation.

Miliband argues that the internal logic of the quasi-market in education created by the ERA, and the particular incentives it offers to parents, demonstrate its divisive tendencies, which he suggests are not only disadvantageous to those pupils in schools which become unpopular, but are 'also suboptimal for society at large'.

As has been suggested above, empowerment of parents could take a number of forms of which choice over school is only one. Though a power of 'exit' (Hirschman, 1970), such as that offered under the ERA may have the coincidental result of increasing parental 'voice', it seems likely that there are other mechanisms which could offer parents 'voice', perhaps more effectively, than the particular 'exit/choice' provisions of the ERA, and possibly without the consequences identified by Ranson and Miliband.

An alternative agenda for choice

Though it is clear from the history set out earlier in this chapter that the voucher agenda in Britain has been one pursued exclusively by certain sections of the political right, Chitty (1992) recounts how Shirley Williams, Secretary of State for education under the last Labour administration, sought to introduce measures aimed at enhancing parental choice in secondary schooling, only to be defeated by influential figures on the left of the Party. However, more recently Le Grand (1989) has considered whether there is an argument for adoption and adaptation of voucher principles by those on the left.

Given a scenario in which all schools were state owned, and in which parents were not able to 'top up' the basic level of funding provided by vouchers, and in which free transport was provided to enable children to travel to a choice of schools, Le Grand suggests that education vouchers could usefully serve essentially socialist ends, while continuing to fulfil the function of rendering schools responsive to parental demand.

However, Le Grand goes on to identify significant problems from a leftist perspective even in as unlikely a scenario as this. He notes that it would not resolve the potentially inegalitarian consequences of oversubscribed schools being able, by whatever means, to select their pupils, and also discusses other problematic aspects of the operation of parental choice. He considers the need to address the lack of information available to parents on which they could make *informed* choices, though notes that any present state of relative ignorance imposed upon many parents may prove to be a result of the existing education system, and would therefore be less problematic in a more socialist environment. He notes also a significant risk that parents may make the 'wrong' choice of school, either because of putting their interests above those of their children, or, 'because their interpretation of what is in their children's interests does not necessarily coincide with the interests of the wider society'.

He notes, in a manner reminiscent of Finch (1984), that,

> Many people argue that education confers external benefits – benefits to society over and above those accruing to the immediate beneficiaries. Thus it is important to instil a common core of specific values and beliefs in each citizen. There may also be wider economic interest in the development of certain skills. Complete freedom of choice by parents could result in a divided society *and* an inefficient economy.
>
> (Le Grand, 1989, p. 201, emphasis added)

Le Grand suggests, as a mechanism for attacking the tendency of the current education system to reproduce, or increase, existing societal inequalities, a process of positive discrimination, whereby the vouchers of those identified as currently disadvantaged would be given an enhanced value, thereby making such pupils *more* attractive than their advantaged counterparts, to schools whose funding was based on pupil numbers.

Though provocative, Le Grand's piece does not make a convincing case for those on the left to pursue an agenda for education based around voucher principles, and, significantly, fails to address adequately the planning issues raised by a voucher model. However, one particularly useful aspect of Le Grand's piece is that it does state clearly a relatively rarely discussed issue; that the interests of parents will not necessarily be the same as those of their children, the problem of 'proxy rights' discussed by Jonathan (1993).

Adler (1990), also considering alternatives to the policies of the present government, gives substantial emphasis to the interests of children. He addresses the central issue raised by Finch, Le Grand and others, of how to resolve the potential conflict between the needs of individual children and those of society, but also takes into account the potential divergence of interest between parents and their children. He notes in a later piece (Adler, 1993) that, as schools differ significantly, it is necessary to pursue an agenda which will 'ensure that children attend those schools which best meet their particular needs', and concludes that, 'In practical terms this suggests that greater attention should be given to *reasons for choice* and that the *existence of choice* should not necessarily determine the outcome' (emphasis added).

Winners and losers

Lewis (1993b) raises 'choice' to the level of a human right, and an essential objective of the political process. He states that 'by providing market-type opportunities citizens will vote their preference in the marketplace'. He notes also that for such an objective to be realized, the choice available must be between a range of quality 'products'. Like Osborne and Gaebler's work (1992), Lewis's writing is informed by a belief in equity. There exists a danger, however, that, in the nature of competition, a competitive market will produce as many, or more, losers than winners. The introduction of a blanket 'right' of choice may produce highly inequitable outcomes.

In stating their intention to consider parents' rights in choosing schools as an opportunity to assess the impact of client's rights on a social welfare programme, Adler *et al.* (1989) point to a number of factors that can undermine the utility of 'rights' in pursuing improved and equitable social welfare provision. Two of these factors seem of particular significance in relation to parent's powers regarding both choice of school, and opting out. They cite Galanter (1975) in support of the proposition that the clients most likely to benefit from such rights are those that are already least disadvantaged. Thus, they suggest, 'rights may limit the ability of social welfare programmes to achieve a reduction in inequalities'.

Secondly, they note that, 'strengthening clients' procedural rights may confer the symbolic appearance of legality on the programmes in question and make it more difficult to achieve fundamental changes that could really enhance social welfare'.

This aspect may be considered particularly relevant in relation to opting out, where case-study evidence, discussed in the next chapter, suggests strongly that though the procedure for parental ballot on opting out is important from the point of view of legitimating the change brought about, the changes do not necessarily produce net gains either in terms of educational standards or substantive influence for parents.

The research findings produced by Adler *et al.* (1989) relating to Scotland, where a stronger form of parental choice, roughly equivalent to that introduced by the ERA, was established in 1981, state that, where significant numbers of parents have chosen to 'exit' the local schools, those children left behind may find the range of available subjects, and other educational opportunities significantly reduced as the resources available to the school are proportionally reduced. They note also that 'there is, as yet, no evidence that the legislation has contributed to an overall improvement in standards'.

This approach seems to bear out the conclusions reached by Meredith (1992) on the parental choice provisions of both the 1980 Act and the ERA. He concludes that both sets of provisions formed 'a parents' charter for a minority of strong-willed, articulate, middle-class parents with the time, inclination and knowledge of the system required to pursue *their* claims to what they see as a satisfactory conclusion' (original stress).

Similar findings are available from the USA, where, as Edwards and Whitty (1992) report, Moore (1990) has noted in relation to the exercise of parental choice in Chicago, the large number of parents who did not seek to exercise choice 'did so with little understanding', while a 'typically middle-class' minority, 'well connected to networks of information and influence', devoted great energy to 'mastering the intricacies of admissions and negotiating the outcomes they wanted'.

The message seems to be that by simply introducing a right of choice, structural inequalities will be replicated, or even heightened. In addition, it seems necessary to state that choices based on inadequate information, a theme returned to later in this and subsequent chapters, really fail to amount to choice at all, and that to introduce a right of choice without facilitating or enabling all consumers to exercise the right equally effectively, is likely, from an egalitarian or equitable point of view, to produce highly undesirable outcomes. The point is expressed lucidly by Jonathan (1993), who observes that 'rights as trumps' tends only to reinforce the position of those who already hold a strong hand.

Choice without markets?

It is difficult to disagree with the central importance attached to choice by Lewis (1993b). However, the consequences identified above of the kind of market forces introduced into education might produce an intuitive reaction against choice as well as against markets. One response to this, and an attempt to introduce perceived benefits of markets without the inequitable outcomes is that of Adler (1993), who seeks to avoid throwing out baby choice along with the bathwater of the market.

Adler advocates structural and procedural reforms resulting in collaborative clusters of schools that provide a range of choice for parents, but within an atmosphere of cooperation rather than competition between institutions, allowing vulnerable schools to be protected and aided. Parents, and older pupils themselves, would be assisted by education professionals to make an informed decision as to the school a child should attend. He suggests a model in which there is significant community input into the school system facilitated by an effective, overarching local authority, comparable perhaps with that introduced in Cambridge, Massachusetts, and with the proposals of Brian Sams, Conservative Chair of the education committee in the London borough of Bexley (Sams, 1991).

Adler admits that such a shift in structure and culture from the present model is unlikely to be achieved easily, but his work at least serves to offer a coherent alternative perspective on choice in education to that of the New Right; an alternative that has hitherto been largely lacking.

Like Brighouse and Tomlinson (1991), Adler is seeking to offer the benefits of quality schooling to all children. The implementation of any such enterprise presupposes a massive, long-term investment in education facilities, and in the meantime, we are faced with continuing to ration the scarce resource of quality schooling via whatever model the government of the day chooses to adopt. A model deriving from the market principles first introduced by the ERA looks likely to be with us for some time.

The consequences of market choice

It is clear that parental participation in education decision making can take a variety of forms, but that only one, choice, has been given effect under the ERA. Evidence from the 1980s and since the ERA tends to suggest that the net effect of this single-track model of parental empowerment is to polarize the issues of choice and planning. The impression is gained that a straightforward choice exists between administration via simple, unconstrained market forces, or, strong bureaucratic planning. Evidence presented in Chapter 3, points clearly towards a conclusion that parental choice, if widely exercised in its present form, seems likely to be incompatible with effective planning of a local system of schools.

It should also be recalled that the justification offered for the introduction of market choice into public education was that it would have the effect of improving educational standards. As stated at the start of this chapter, the whole concept of educational standards proves enormously difficult to pin-down. Before turning to examine, briefly, the question of school effectiveness and evaluation, it seems necessary to reiterate the key consequences of choice that have been identified.

Choice has primarily been manifested under the ERA in parental choice of school, and the choice to opt-out of LEA control, both themes returned to in the empirical evidence presented in Chapter 4, which raises substantial doubts as to the extent to which parents have in fact been meaningfully empowered.

There is strong evidence to suggest that only a minority of parents have in practice been able to encash such rights, and that where they have, this has had negative knock-on effects for those less able or willing to pursue their claims.

The end-product of this process has been the reallocation of that scarce and precious commodity, quality education, in favour of those already relatively advantaged. As Chitty (1992) has put it, 'some parents are more knowledgeable, more influential and more articulate than others. They bring to the marketplace certain clear advantages. They know how to "play the system" and win.'

STANDARDS

Where does this highway go to?

I have stated repeatedly that the fundamental claim of those who introduced and supported the ERA reforms was that the introduction of market mechanisms into education, and the resulting competitive pressures on schools to attract pupils, would lead to higher educational standards. While Lewis argues for choice as a human right, and therefore as in a sense an end in itself, in the context of the ERA choice must be viewed as a route to be followed in order to reach a destination. So, where does this highway go to?

In the course of attaching to consumer choice both the role of primary accountability mechanism and the major decision-making force, what I identified as a secondary function of accountability mechanisms, quality assurance, has taken on a pre-eminent position. 'Choice' is said to be the answer to 'How do we render power holders accountable?', and 'account-ability' the answer to 'How do we improve standards?' Thus, in considering choice as the highway to improvement, we need some conception of what the destination is, for if not, how will we know when we have arrived, or even if we are heading in the correct direction?

In assessing the effectiveness of a policy initiative, it is necessary to con-sider input, output and outcomes. Lewis (1993b, p. 12) offers a simple illustration: 'if the inputs in the police service are more resources, the outputs more arrests and the outcomes less crime then the fact of more arrests having no impact on levels of crime suggests the abandonment of existing policies'. In terms of schooling, if the policy maker decides that the input will be choice, the output will be competition, and the outcome will be higher educational standards, it should be difficult for the policy maker to justify their policy choice if they cannot point towards improved standards. The problem, as stated at the start of this chapter, is that the measurement of educational outcome, in terms of standards, is no easy task.

So, how do we know when we've got there?

Only five years after the introduction of major educational reforms, it is, of course, rather early to seek a definitive answer as to whether they have produced the desired outcome. However, if we are ever to be able to assess the reforms in terms of their professed aims, it is necessary to devise mechan-isms for defining and assessing standards and improvements. There is no doubt that the input of a form of choice, and output of competition have happened, but has the desired outcome also resulted?

If we are to avoid glib responses, based on impressionistic or partial evidence, we will need explicit and objective measures that can be system-atically applied.

Mortimore (1992) notes how in recent debates on the reform of education, discussions of 'quality control' and 'standards' are often 'premised more on rhetoric than on evidence'. He notes the potential for a range of sources to be used in monitoring quality, including HMI and other inspectorates, the use of tests and examinations, the judgement of parents, and academic research.

He believes however, that recent public discussions of educational stan-dards have been 'confused and unhelpful', and that the kind of simple league table produced for parents following the Parent's Charter and Education (Schools) Act 1992, 'could mask considerable under-achievement or, alternatively, conceal genuine school effectiveness'. In his judgement, rather than giving meaningful information on quality of schooling, such tables provide instead 'a good indication of the background and amount of prior learning of pupils'.

Though presented primarily as a means of facilitating parental choice, the publication of school league tables, based on raw results from children's performances in public examination is the principle measure of educational standards so far produced by the government. It is perhaps indicative of the level of development of government policy in the area.

As a means of informing choice, the tables have been criticized from many quarters as revealing little about the effect of schooling, and rather more about the intake of schools. Put simply, schools that recruit an intake above average in terms of educational and social advantage are likely to produce better examination results at the end of the schooling process. The boycott by teachers of Key Stage 3 tests in 1993 was objectively justified in terms of the perceived poor design of the particular tests, though it also probably reflected deeper concerns regarding the role of such testing in providing the information for the compilation of league tables, in order to further competition.

A large part of such criticism derives from the argument that such tests are essentially summative rather than formative: their purpose is to assess pupils achievement against a common standard, and, when assembled on a school-by-school basis, to allow comparisons to be made between schools. As such, they lack the formative, or diagnostic, purpose that, it is argued, should underlie testing in education: the identification of children's strengths, weaknesses and needs that can be responded to in the next stage of the educational process.

As with the testing of pupils, so with the summative testing of schools by reference to their pupils results: they will be used simply to describe a level of performance rather than as a mechanism for identifying needs in order that resources may be allocated to effect improvements. Indeed in practice, under existing arrangements, resources will flow to schools demonstrating the greatest strength rather than those with the greatest need for improvement.

There is no doubt, however, that such league tables have certain attractions, most obviously their accessibility. Their danger lies in their tendency, in their present form to oversimplify. Thus, in this respect, if techniques can be developed to analyse the effect a school has on its pupils, the 'value added' factor, then this would address the first complaint. The second complaint, regarding the use to which assessments are put, remains. Might it not be argued that a school which is under-performing when compared with its competitors should receive such support and resources as would enable it to improve, rather than facing the loss of resources that will occur if parents identify it as an under-performer, and therefore send their children elsewhere?

However, this fails to assist us in our task of working out how to identify if standards are improving. Though the standard of public debate has generally been sadly lacking in this respect, a substantial amount of detailed research and discussion has taken place among educationists.

A useful collection of material, summarizing much recent British research in this area is edited by Riddell and Brown (1991). They explicitly state that much learning is done outside of school, and that therefore it is necessary to separate clearly school-based outcomes from the influence of external, environmental factors when evaluating a school's performance. In essence, Riddell and Brown identify four matters that must be addressed when carrying out school effectiveness research.

They state that clear *objectives* are required in terms of what is to be evaluated. That is, a statement of what is to be assessed. Among the core areas identified by researchers as valuable indicators in the evaluation of school performance are, 'academic progress, other outcomes and forms of progress, teaching processes, key resources and equal opportunities'. Clearly, some of these are rather more easily measured than others, however, the message is that a holistic approach must be taken if a fuller picture of the school is to be obtained. They offer as an example, the possibility that 'a school with a reputation for high academic standards may pay insufficient attention to its learning support programme or to fostering social awareness among its pupils'.

Secondly, they state that *criteria* must be established against which attainment of these objectives will be measured. Clearly, criteria other than examination results must be considered if a broad impression of the school's performance is to be obtained.

Thirdly, it will be necessary to establish what *evidence* will be used to determine whether these criteria have been fulfilled. Again, an analysis of examination results may not provide sufficiently subtle or precise evidence in respect of these criteria.

Fourthly, it will be necessary to determine how best to *communicate* the findings of the evaluation. In Riddell and Brown's terms, 'Although it is important not to distort evidence by presenting it too superficially, by the same token there is no point in presenting parents with lengthy and highly detailed reports which will not be read.'

While the model established by Riddell and Brown by no means sets out to offer all the answers as to how school performance can be assessed, it at least suggests an analytic framework within which the task can be undertaken. Their work is, however, informed by an essentially formative approach. Thus, if improvements are to be brought about, a detailed understanding of the intake, the school processes, and the outcomes in a broad sense will be necessary. This is not the approach that seems to underlie recent reforms, which have wholly failed to develop the kinds of concepts of objectives, criteria, evidence and communication referred to by Riddell and Brown. Clearly, the development and implementation of a system based on such principles is difficult to achieve, though by no means impossible to move towards, given a will to evaluate schools for formative purposes; instead, the approach has been informed by an entirely summative objective. Schools are to be assessed as a means of enabling parents to choose between them, rather than to identify and address areas for improvement. It is a means of enhancing competition; of identifying 'good' and 'bad' schools; of identifying winners and losers, both among the schools, and among the children.

How far have we got?

Clearly the recent reforms have not gone far down the road towards developing and furthering processes aimed at enabling school effectiveness to be measured in a complete way. As expressed by Longley (1993) considering similar issues in the context of recent reforms of the NHS, the focus has been on readily accessible, 'technical and tangible' rather than more complex, abstract, issues.

Choice, such as it is, will be informed by a partial and potentially misleading set of statistics reflecting only one aspect of the outcome of schools' performances, that is pupils' performances in public tests and examinations, without even any correction for 'value added'.

Schools that perform relatively badly against this indicator, rather than being given the resources to effect improvements, will, if parents choose to send their children elsewhere, be deprived of the basic unit of resource, and will be likely to enter an unstoppable process of decline, taking the children at the school with them. Meanwhile, those schools that perform well against such an indicator, perhaps because of their relatively advantaged intake, whether or not they are under-performing in terms of 'value added' or any broader assessment, will in turn be popular and will be proportionally better resourced. Indeed, a school that is oversubscribed, will, by reference to whatever criteria apply to that school, be able to select and reject applicants for admission.

The issues of choice, selection and school performance will be returned to in the next chapter, when empirical data will be used to demonstrate current trends. In the present context, it is sufficient to note that within the GM sector, where schools are better resourced, both because of popularity with parents and by virtue of the enhanced funding attached to GM status, early evidence suggests that these schools are not performing better than their LEA maintained neighbours against current criteria (Halpin *et al.* 1991;

Ofsted, 1993). This suggests that market forces are not having the effect of causing popular schools to improve, but that if funding differentials continue, less popular, and less well-resourced schools will enter a vicious circle: unpopularity leads to fewer resources, leads to less popularity, leads to fewer resources, leads to less popularity . . .

As with parents seeking to exercise choice, certain schools have in-built advantages which will tend to make them winners in the competitive marketplace; others will be losers.

PUBLIC LAW AND THE EDUCATION ENTERPRISE

This chapter, concerned with the concepts underpinning discussions of the management of a public education system has revolved around the concept of 'choice'. It has been considered as a mechanism of accountability, as a means of enhancing educational standards, and, as a valuable human right in itself.

It is worth recalling that Ranson and Stewart (1989), in considering the role of management in the public sector note that the essence of political discourse regarding the distribution of a public good is the exercise of collective choice. Similarly, in arguing for choice as a vital aspect of the public enterprise, Lewis (1993b) notes that 'it is important to understand that markets need to be shaped, regulation enforced, ground rules observed and *collective values set*' (emphasis added).

A fundamental problem arises as to how to provide choice, both in a collective sense, and, for individuals as individuals and as members of a collective body or community. This is demonstrated by the tipping effect described by Miliband (1991), and the impact of the exercise of movements away from unpopular schools identified by Adler *et al.* (1989). Such outcomes, likely to be contrary to collective interests such as equity, are the result of the exercise of individual choice, which, in the existing market model, is given pre-eminence.

Indeed, the development of choice in this context, the 'right' of individual choice becoming a 'trump', appears likely to have an outcome of reinforcing, or even exaggerating existing societal inequalities or hierarchies. The preeminence given to such a right creates an imbalance in the relationship inherent in the concept of citizenship between the position of an individual *qua* individual, and their role as a member of a community. Rather, it is likely to produce outcomes that diminish the sense of equity that attaches to the notion of community.

Lewis (1993b), like Osborne and Gaebler (1992), emphasize the central requirement of equity in the distribution of a public good, and, the idea that if markets cannot, or do not deliver, then a collectively determined agenda, the outcome of some other form of rational discourse, must be relied upon. The role of an individual *as a member of the community* is thus emphasized.

Once community is emphasized, the citizen acquires the right to participate in it, and in its decision-making processes. In a similar way, an individual institution such as a school, can be said to have an interest in actively participating in a local education system, rather than behaving entirely as an isolated atomic body.

The quasi-market in education clearly emphasizes the individual *as* an individual; the possibilities of participation at school level, other than as consumer, are rejected. The emphasis on the individual exclusively as consumer, denies her the right to participate fully in the community, for the process of discourse begins not only at the school gates, when the individual arrives, voucher in hand, as consumer, but much earlier, in the setting of goals for the education system, in establishing structures, in the institutional arrangements for the distribution of that part of the common wealth that is invested in a public good such as education. Empowering citizens with a right of choice, when the right has been substantially abrogated by prior decisions in which they have had no part, denies individuals the right they acquire as part of the community. The balance between representative and participative decision making sought by Ranson and Stewart (1989) is not achieved.

If we return to the fundamental constitutional purpose identified in Chapter 1, of establishing a framework, an arena, within which legitimate processes of decision making can take place, evidence, referred to above, and presented in some detail in the next two chapters, suggests that this constitutional goal is being poorly served by present arrangements. Discourse in this context presupposes processes of extensive, timely, informed and influential participation. If individuals are not enabled to take part in such a process, the legitimacy of the processes is fundamentally undermined. In the role of institutional designer, it is for the public lawyer to address such issues, to assess weaknesses in the present structure, and to suggest improvements.

While this chapter has concerned itself primarily with conceptual issues, the next two focus rather on the observable manifestations of institutional defects, in both the educational and more general institutional edifices of Britain. It is now time to move from broad concepts to fine detail, but, the former must be viewed in the context of the latter, just as the form of administrative law is heavily dependent on the over-arching constitutional arrangements.

Chapter 3 considers empirical data on the functioning of the schools system. Chapter 4 will consider the range of legal interventions in the schools process. In Chapter 5, we shall return to some of the themes I have discussed here, to consider again how public law might fulfil its role in ensuring that the education system lives up to our constitutional expectations.

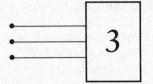

THE MARKET IN SCHOOLS: CHOICE, COMPETITION AND CONTROL

SOURCES OF EVIDENCE

It is now time to consider the outcomes of the reform agenda detailed in the previous two chapters. The evidence cited derives mostly from empirical research into opting-out, arguably the central feature of the ERA measures, and the one that most emphasizes the familiar issues of choice and accountability.

Since the publication of the 1992 White Paper (DFE, 1992) it has been obvious to anyone who cares to consider the future of British schooling that opting-out is intended to be the key measure in bringing about the restructuring of the administrative structure. If schools opt out at the levels projected in the White Paper, LEAs will soon reach the point at which powers begin to be transferred to the FAS, and, in due course, when 75 per cent of schools in their area have obtained GM status, will lose all remaining powers. This scenario presupposes that the flow of opting-out will increase dramatically, which is by no means certain; but the government's intention is at least now clear.

For some time, there was no clear endgame for opting-out. From the outset, there had been doubts within government, even public differences between then Prime Minister Thatcher and her Secretary of State Baker, as to whether opting-out would be the norm or the exception. However, even in the early days, when there was no more than a trickle of schools seeking

GM status, opting-out was already playing a crucial role in reshaping the balance of power. GM schools, and the small number of CTCs, did indeed constitute a breach in the perceived existing LEA monopoly of influence over state schooling, and had an immediate impact on the ability of LEAs to act effectively.

From the late 1970s, LEAs had been under increasing pressure to remove surplus school places, in response to demographic trends and heightened financial stringency. The principle mechanism available to them was to reorganize provision, usually involving the closure or amalgamation of schools, or new post-16 arrangements. As soon as the potential for opting-out arose, it acted as an obstacle to such reorganizations, for what more natural reaction for a school threatened with closure, or unwanted reorganization, than to seek to opt out of the LEA and preserve its present status?

In addition, opting-out served to ensure the operation of a market in state school provision. Any degree of meaningful parental choice involves the availability of surplus capacity, and if LEAs were allowed to act, in the interests of educational and economic efficiency, to remove surplus places, any semblance of choice would be removed. Thus, opting-out, or its potential, has acted as a crucial block on the removal of surplus capacity, and has helped to preserve the appearance of choice.

Much of the evidence presented in this Chapter arises from my doctoral research into the impact of schools opting-out to GM status, carried out between 1989 and 1992, described in detail elsewhere (Feintuck, 1993). Fieldwork took the form of case-studies of six LEA areas, in the course of which a range of interested parties, including headteachers, governors, LEA members and officers, parents' representatives and trade union officials were interviewed, and documents scrutinized. Material gathered from interviews with representatives of national bodies with an active interest in opting-out, including the DFE, Grant Maintained Schools Centre (GMSC), Choice in Education (CIE), and Local Schools Information (LSI), is also referred to, as is a postal questionnaire completed by officers from 80 per cent of LEAs in England and Wales.

Although this research forms the main body of evidence referred to in this chapter, reference is also made to research on the GM sector carried out by, or on behalf of, other bodies, including LSI and the Assistant Masters and Mistresses Association (AMMA), and, relating specifically to the issue of standards, a recent report by the Office for Standards in Education (Ofsted, 1993). The chapter also draws on recent research focused on other aspects of the ERA reforms, especially work relating to the impact of open enrolment, and the introduction of CTCs.

CHOICE IN SCHOOLING

Advocates of the recent reforms point towards two main manifestations of parental empowerment within ERA. The first claim is that, as a result of the measures relating to open enrolment to schools, parents are now able to exert direct choice over the school their child will attend. The second is that, via the mechanism of opting-out, parents are able to choose between leaving a school under the control of the LEA (though in reality local authority control is greatly diminished under LMS), and, having the school leave the LEA, to be funded instead direct from central government as a GM school.

Choice of school

The introduction of open enrolment to schools under ERA represented, in theory at least, an attempt to reduce the control exercised by LEAs over the allocation of school places, while enhancing the degree of choice available to parents. Though Section 76 of the 1944 Act had introduced a requirement to take into account parental preference, and this aspect had been confirmed by the provisions of the 1980 Act, the practical outcomes of these measures had left a minority of parents dissatisfied with the degree of choice available to them. Introduced by the ERA, the concept of open enrolment was said to be bolstered by the publication, following the Parent's Charter and Education (Schools) Act 1992, of league tables of schools' performances rated by reference to the performance of pupils in external examinations.

The validity of such data in assessing the performance of schools has already been questioned in Chapter 2. Such information is claimed to provide parents with the necessary information on which they can base a decision as to which school they would like their child to attend. However, the complexity of comparing school effectiveness is well illustrated in many studies, including those by Brighouse and Tomlinson (1991) and Riddell and Brown (1991), and there now appears to be a gradual acceptance, even by natural allies of education markets, that raw test data is unlikely to be adequate as a primary source of information for parents.

Bash and Coulby (1989) locate the move to a quasi-market in education clearly within a broad trend towards individualism at the expense of collective goals. The Bristol Polytechnic Education Study Group (in Bash and Coulby, 1989) suggest that the move to open enrolment has no justification (given that they state 95 per cent of children already attended the school chosen by their parents) other than as part of the ERA package, in which its structural importance, as the driving mechanism for LMS, is crucial. They see a significant risk of it leading to 'selection by the back door' and potential for furthering racial segregation. Simon (1992) points towards evidence from Scotland (Echols *et al.*, 1990) as indicating that such measures for parental choice 'by circumventing or distorting comprehensive education, are recreating, in a new mode, the inequalities and divisions of the past'.

Research findings presented by Elliot (1982) and Johnson (1990), indicate that in any case, 'parental choice of school is most strongly influenced by pragmatic and pastoral considerations, factors which direct little attention, if any, to the actual structure of what the child will receive by way of educational content or method at the selected school' (Johnson, 1990, quoting Petch, 1986). Bastow (1991) confirms this, finding that a school's performance, as demonstrated in exam results, was not one of sixteen variables identified as being used by parents when choosing between schools.

Adler *et al.* (1989) survey the outcomes of the introduction of a level of choice, broadly similar to that introduced in England and Wales by the ERA, into Scotland in 1981. Their research indicates that in Scotland, although the number of placing requests increased during the 1980s, nine out of every ten children still attend their local school, and that the exercise of choice via placing requests has largely been limited to urban areas, presumably where practical choice actually exists. They find, however, that where significant numbers of parents have chosen to 'exit' their local schools, 'the loss of some pupils has, in the case of some under-enrolled schools, left other pupils in a very exposed position', the very tipping effect identified by Miliband (1991), referred to in Chapter 2.

Not only is choice therefore being exercised by a relatively small number of parents, but it is also, according to Meredith (1992), proving to be only a parent's charter for those assertive, articulate, middle-class parents who choose or are able to exercise their new 'right'.

In Walford's terms,

> Without being condescending to the many working-class and ethnic minority parents who continually fight against the odds to achieve a good education for their children, we must accept that on average working-class parents and the parents of most ethnic minorities are less knowledgeable about their children's education than is the average white middle class parent. They are likely to have had poorer educational experiences themselves, with little experience of further or higher education. They are also likely to be less able to negotiate educational bureaucracies or to present themselves as 'supportive' parents in interview with head teachers or other selectors, who are themselves mostly white and middle class.
>
> (Walford, 1990, p. 79)

A further set of issues arises out of the 'proxy' nature of choice embodied in recent educational reform. Jonathan (1993) and Adler (1993) both refer to the potential for parental perceptions of the interests of their children to differ from the children's or other alternative versions of a child's best interests. The legislative focus on parents is, however, largely reflected in research into the exercise of choice over schools, though recent research by West and Varlaam (1991), focusing on pupils' perception of choice, suggests that children may well bring somewhat different criteria to the exercise of choice to those of their parents. Walford's research into CTCs (Walford, 1991) also suggests that children often play a crucial role in the selection of secondary schools.

Adler's reform proposals include a limited empowering of older children in the exercise of choice, though within the context of a system in which the LEA and teachers are able to play an active role as information centre and facilitator of choice, reflecting the kind of model employed in Cambridge, Massachusetts, referred to by Sky (1992). This model suggests a continuing role for the LEA, not only in bolstering the ability of individual children to influence their own future, but also in the provision of a valuable resource serving the educational interests of the community as a whole, including equity in the delivery of educational services. Whether LEAs are in modern times able to fulfil such functions, acting in support of a local education system and as a counterbalance to the consequences of atomized parental choice is debatable (Cordingley and Kogan, 1993).

Such community issues would include racial segregation, a matter specifically allowed to override programmes for parental choice in the United States. Racial or religious segregation clearly becomes a very real possibility as a consequence of any effective exercise of parental choice. In Britain, *causes célèbres* such as the 'Dewsbury Affair', and the case of the Cleveland mother who sought to move her child to a predominantly 'White' school (see *R v Cleveland CC* ex parte *Commission for Racial Equality* (1992), The Times, 25 August 1992) catch the headlines from time-to-time. However, debates over separatism in education have been most obvious in relation to the possibility of state-funding for Muslim schools, in the same way as support is given to other religious groups such as voluntary-aided Anglican, Roman Catholic, Methodist and Jewish schools. In this sense, the potential for choice of state-funded education in accordance with religious beliefs appears still more arbitrary. Early in 1991 it was reported (*Education*, 15 March 1991) that the potential for hundreds of applications for voluntary-aided status from Muslim groups was a major problem for Kenneth Clarke, then Secretary of State, who wished to encourage voluntary-aided CTCs.

Additional factors suggesting moves towards exclusivity in schooling are indicated into research into the selection of pupils, and weeding-out of identified 'problem cases' such as those referred to in relation to Queen Elizabeth School for Boys (QEB), Barnet, in Chapter 4, and the adoption of a policy of not admitting blind pupils by a new GM school in Waltham Forest, reversing a previous policy of cooperation with a nearby 'special' school (*The Guardian* 24 July 1993).

Similarly, moves towards specialization by schools, proposed in the 1992 White Paper, and confirmed by Education Minister Lady Blatch (*The Guardian*, 16 December 1992) in the form of allowing schools to select up to 10 per cent of pupils based on aptitude in particular subject areas, especially technology, suggests a significant breach in the theory of comprehensive intake.

Potential conflicts between diversity and equity in the provision of schooling are obvious and very relevant. However, in reality, the differences between most state schools, including GM schools and CTCs, can generally be reduced to differences in ethos, esteem and funding rather than the provision of distinctive curricula provision. Recent research carried out in Kirklees, West Yorkshire, demonstrates that parents are well aware of the irony created by the ERA, at the same time as claiming to further parental choice, introducing a centrally prescribed National Curriculum, that acts as a significant limit on the amount of choice that can be made available by schools to parents (*TES*, 18 June 1993).

Given practical problems of home to school travel, it is obvious also that any meaningful degree of choice is only likely to be available to those living in urban centres. As Echols *et al.* (1990) have demonstrated in the Scottish context, the degree of choice diminishes as the distance of alternative schools from the home increases. In most rural areas, there is therefore unlikely to be a range of viable alternatives to the nearest secondary school.

The recent reforms relating to parental choice appear to have gone the same way as earlier choice-centred initiatives which have failed to empower parents significantly, and indeed, contrary to principles of equity, have furthered a hierarchical system of schooling. The controversial Assisted Places scheme, introduced in the Education Act 1980, intended to allow access to private schooling for children of families of limited means via the provision of means tested state funding, appears to have been subverted to the end of preserving hierarchy, with the scheme in practice being utilized by predominantly middle-class families (Whitty *et al.*, 1989).

Indeed, it appears that for many parents choice of school retains a certain chimeral quality. It is clear that parental choice depends on surplus places being available at desirable schools, and as is confirmed in my study of GM schools, once the school becomes oversubscribed, the element of choice is transferred to those in power at the school, rather than parents of would-be pupils. Simon (1992) quotes a document produced by the Advisory Centre for Education (ACE) as saying of parents that in reality, 'They do not have a choice, they have a preference – that is all', and presents a range of other evidence leading him to conclude that 'all is not well on the "parental choice" front'.

Like ACE, the Association of Metropolitan Authorities (AMA) reports an increase in appeals against decisions on admissions. Steve Byers, AMA education chair, has recently attributed this rise to the fact that 'Parents' hopes are being raised by misleading ministerial statements', and added that 'Their hopes are being dashed' (*TES*, 31 July 1992).

In 1992, *Education* (17 April 1992) discussed these problems in the context of the Parent's Charter, and stressed the problems created by 'The Hillingdon Syndrome', referring to the London Borough in which more than half the secondary schools had acquired GM status, thereby undermining any attempts to devise a centrally planned or coordinated admissions system. In such a situation, parental choice is likely to be subject to severe restrictions as a consequence of the limited number of places available at the most popular schools. For Hillingdon residents, as in other London Boroughs (*The Guardian*, 4 August 1992) containing a number of 'popular' schools, an added factor to be considered is the potentially significant influx of children from neighbouring boroughs, given the impact of the 'Greenwich Ruling' (*R v Greenwich LBC* ex parte *Governors of John Ball School* (1990) 88 LGR 589) which has the effect of rendering unlawful attempts, when allocating school places, to discriminate in favour of residents within the borough at the expense of pupils from outside the borough.

There is therefore, a very real sense in which parental choice can be reduced to something approaching a lottery. However, there may also be a risk, as Lawton (1989) indicates, that where choice is given effect, 'minority interests are fostered' and that 'the quality of education for the majority is not being improved', or, as Echols *et al.* (1990) conclude, findings 'confirm the fundamental sociological tenet that voluntary individual behaviour is socially structured in ways that reproduce persistent inequalities between groups'.

A recent briefing paper from the National Commission on Education (1993) summarizes the situation as follows:

- The evidence from a decade of open enrolment in Scotland suggests that parental choice has led to an inefficient use of resources, widening disparities between schools, increased social segregation and threats to equality of educational opportunity.
- The gains achieved by some pupils have been more than offset by the losses incurred by others and by the community as a whole.
- It is likely that the outcomes of open enrolment in England will be even more problematic.
- Recent legislation has not achieved an optimal balance between the rights of parents to choose schools for their children and the responsibilities of government to promote the education of all children.

What seems clear in addition, is that the particular model of parental empowerment, in the form of limited choice, embodied in recent legislation, is not only largely superficial, but serves to polarize the issues of choice and planning, effectively offering them as mutually exclusive alternatives.

The 1992 White Paper offers little more than pious hopes of cooperation between GM schools and LEAs as a remedy for the Hillingdon Syndrome. Whether the new quangos will ultimately be empowered to carry out effective planning, including control over admissions, is uncertain, though it seems necessary for someone to perform such functions. It is also necessary that whoever ultimately acquires such responsibilities should be accountable in the exercise of their powers.

Choosing to opt out

As with the choice of schools, any analysis of the degree of choice introduced by opting-out begs a number of other questions regarding the nature and location of choice. In particular, it is necessary to inquire into who in practice exercises such choice, and what changes the exercise of choice actually brings about.

An examination of the text of the relevant ERA provisions, even if combined with a study of official guidance on the subject in the form of DFE Circulars and other publications, reveals only a partial picture of the realities of opting-out.

Sections 52 to 104 of the ERA set out the processes for the acquisition of GM status and the arrangements for managing GM schools after incorporation. The funding arrangements are outlined in the Act, but detailed in the Finance Regulations, published, to date, annually.

The statute established that if either, the governing body of a school resolves on two separate occasions to seek GM status (though the 1993 Act has now abolished the requirement of a second resolution, in the interests of streamlining the opt-out process), or, if a petition is received signed by 20 per cent of parents of current pupils at the school seeking GM status, the governing body must make arrangements for a ballot of all parents of currently registered pupils to be held, asking whether the school should opt out. If a majority of parents vote in favour of opting-out, the governing body must then prepare a formal proposal to seek GM status, which is forwarded to the Secretary of State. If, however, less than 50 per cent of eligible parents vote at the ballot, the result will not stand, and a second ballot, based on the same franchise must be held. On the second occasion, a majority decision will determine the issue, regardless of turnout.

The formal application for GM status must include details of the proposed governing body for the school, and include detail of such matters as admissions arrangements. On receipt of a formal proposal, and having allowed time for representations to be made regarding the application, the Secretary of State may approve or reject the application, or approve it in amended form. By virtue of Section 73 (4), if the GM application is on the table at the same time as an LEA reorganization proposal concerning the school, the Secretary of State must consider the two proposals alongside each other, but reach a decision on the opt-out proposal first.

Section 89 establishes a formal procedure that GM schools must go through if they wish to make a 'significant change of character' to the school. Such changes, including for example a move from comprehensive to selective intake, or a change from co-educational to single-sex provision, require the approval of the Secretary of State. At the time of the Bill's passage through Parliament, the then Secretary of State Kenneth Baker gave an undertaking that no such changes of character would be considered by him within five years of a school opting-out, however, by 1992 the new Secretary of State, Kenneth Clarke, had declared that he would no longer consider himself bound by the undertaking, a position now confirmed in the White Paper (DFE, 1992, para. 7.9).

From this outline of the provisions relating to opting-out, it would appear that parents of present pupils have a central part in the process, potentially commencing it by petition, and ratifying the course of action via the ballot. In practice, however, evidence indicates that only a minority of opt-out bids arise out of parental petition, the majority being started by resolutions of the governing body. Indeed, case-study material suggests strongly that the majority of opt-out bids are started, and driven by the headteacher, and/or a small group of governors, and that the views of teachers generally, but the head teacher in particular, are often crucial in persuading parents to vote for or against a proposal (Feintuck, 1993).

In addition, the role of the Secretary of State, with the ability to reject opt-out bids supported by parents at the ballot, or to approve a bid in the face of only relatively weak parental support, has proved to be a crucial, and highly contentious aspect of the process.

This latter issue, is highlighted in the cases of approval of GM status for Stratford School in Labour controlled Newham where a bare majority of parents voting at the second ballot (less than 35 per cent of all eligible parents) voted in favour, while Walsingham School, in the Conservative 'flagship' authority of Wandsworth, had an application for GM status rejected in the face of overwhelming parental support for the move. Such cases emphasize the crucial importance attaching to the exercise of discretion by the Secretary of State, explored more fully in Chapter 4 in the context of litigation arising out of the opt out of Beechen Cliff School in the city of Bath.

However, critics of opting-out have often focused their opposition to the opt-out process around what they consider to be the fundamentally undemocratic nature of the franchise for opt-out ballots. A constant criticism of the opt-out process has been the narrowness of the electorate for the opt-out ballot, in only enfranchising parents of present pupils, and not even requiring consultation with other affected parties. To the general criticisms, founded in a belief in local democracy, can be added more specifically the absurdity of parents of children presently in the fifth or upper-sixth form, and therefore about to leave the school (or indeed having left, as at the second ballot in the celebrated case of Stratford School, discussed shortly) being entitled to vote, while parents of future pupils (or indeed the new first year at the time of the Stratford second ballot) being given no say in the school's future.

The legitimacy of a decision arrived at in such a situation is obviously highly questionable, and where a tiny minority occurs on a second ballot, amid strongly supported accusations of ballot-rigging, as at Stratford, such doubts are substantially compounded.

An additional aspect of the opt-out process is the degree to which those voting are adequately informed as to the consequences of their decision. If the occurrence of meaningful choice is dependent upon the provision of adequate information to allow the person said to be so empowered to be able to exercise *informed* choice, then evidence from several case studies suggests that parents do not have sufficient information as to enable this precondition of choice to be fulfilled.

The testimony of the Chair of the Parents' Association at one high-profile GM school is particularly relevant in this respect. She referred specifically to the failure to explain adequately to parents, both before and after the opt-out, what the consequences of GM status would be. She also explicitly referred to the failure to provide any information to parties outside enfranchised parents, for example parents of children at feeder schools.

The quality of debate surrounding individual opt-out bids is remarkably inconsistent. In some cases, LEAs have actively cooperated with schools in providing written information to, and arranging meetings for parents. Sometimes opt-out bids have taken place in an atmosphere of hostility between LEA and school, either overt or covert. Sometimes these meetings and other consultation processes have been extended to involve the wider community, including on occasion representatives of feeder schools. Sometimes representatives of opposing lobby groups, such as the CIE and LSI have been invited; sometimes only one side has attended, sometimes neither.

In so far as a general trend can be discerned, the debate on opting-out has largely been focused closely on the parents of present pupils at the school, to the exclusion of interest groups in the wider community. Given the franchise at opt-out ballots, this is hardly surprising, and neither the statutory procedures nor DFE guidance require or advocate more extensive consultation.

The problems created by lack of accurate and complete information can be exacerbated in situations such as those at Stratford, where all accounts seem to suggest a multiplicity of motives underlying the opt-out, causing a high degree of confusion over what the opt-out meant. This may well have contributed substantially to the divisive battle that took place in the school after the acquisition of GM status. It certainly seems that a small group of governors believed that GM status allowed them, claiming to be representative of parents, to run the school free of interference either from the headteacher or external influences.

The circumstances at Eckington School in Derbyshire were in some ways similar. Although the primary cause of the opt-out move to save the school's sixth-form was similar to the apparent proximate cause of Stratford's move (saving the school from closure), Eckington's headteacher found that the situation had in essence been reduced to a simple party political struggle between Labour and Conservative supporters, with the subtleties of the move lost. Likewise, a senior education officer at Derbyshire LEA saw the other, earlier, opt-out moves in the county as being surrounded with 'Save Our School' sentiment. Though it could be claimed that the active campaigning by teachers and other local groups to avert the opt-out were ultimately successful in informing the electorate at Eckington, this could be seen merely as successful propagandizing, and in any event, this cannot necessarily be considered a typical campaign.

The abiding impression from the case-study evidence is that a wide range of agendas can exist for opting-out, as exemplified by the different factors present within the Birmingham opt-outs, where one school has obtained GM status exclusively as a reaction to uncertainty over its future within the LEA maintained sector, while another opted out specifically to obtain greater flexibility of management, and, because of the potential offered by GM status for obtaining greater resources (Feintuck, 1993, ch. 7). Similar degrees of contrast can be seen throughout case-study material. Equally, as Beechen Cliff and Stratford illustrate respectively, it is possible to have a poorly informed electorate or one with no clearly identified rationale for taking a decision to opt out.

Ultimately, the case-study material suggests strongly that, even within the narrow franchise for opt-out ballots, the existing opt-out procedure does not ensure that those who vote on opting-out are provided with sufficient information to allow them to make an informed and meaningful choice.

The range of motives for opting-out can be broadly categorized into three groups:

- Opt-outs deriving from a threat to the schools future arising out of LEA reorganization proposals to either close, or restructure the school.
- Opt-outs motivated by the attraction of financial advantages attached to GM status.
- Opt-outs arising out of more abstract causes, such as long-term dissatisfaction with LEA management, or a general wish for more independence.

Though the first of these factors appears to be the most common proximate cause of opt-out bids, and best demonstrates the structural importance
of opting-out, the second factor appears to have been increasingly to the
fore in the minds of headteachers and governors considering a move to GM
status.

Evidence has mounted over the years since 1988 that substantial financial
advantages attach to opting-out, hardening from a general impression in the
early days to a hard fact, acknowledged by government ministers in more
recent times. The advantages accruing have been principally in the area
of capital grants, though significant gains are also to be found in terms of
Special Purpose Grants, and grants for restructuring made available to GM
schools in the first year after opting-out. However, the Finance Regulations
have also provided an additional cash bonus for GM schools in the form of
a 'top-up' to the AMG, initially of 16 per cent, later reduced to 15 per cent,
meant to represent funding to allow the GM school to purchase services
previously supplied by the relevant LEA. This sum, along with the Annual
Maintenance Grant (AMG), is recouped from the LEA. Not only does
this allow GM schools more room for manoeuvre in terms of expenditure
priorities (for example, spending on books or other facilities, or refurbish-
ment, rather than on teacher training or other support services), but also,
according to LEA sources, amounts to a straightforward bonus, it being
estimated that the real amount needed to compensate GM schools for the
replacement of LEA centrally provided services is only around 11 per cent
(Feintuck, 1993, ch. 12).

With such attractive advantages, it would hardly be surprising if schools
were persuaded that opting-out was in their interests, especially in a period in
which local authority expenditure is under increasingly stringent constraints.

Opting-out has, to date, been concentrated in relatively few LEA areas,
largely in the south-east of England. Survey data (Feintuck, 1993 and Local
Schools Information, 1992) reveals a direct correlation between opting-out
and political control at a local level. Data demonstrate a clear trend for levels
of opting-out to be highest in Conservative controlled county councils.
Indeed, further consideration of the LSI figures demonstrates that half (98
out of 196) of the GM schools operating, approved, or 'minded to approve'
at the time of their survey are from within nine LEAs, all of which are
Conservative controlled, and all, apart from the two London Boroughs of
Bromley and Hillingdon, are county councils.

If the link were simply between Conservative control and opting-out, then
the causal factor may obviously be thought to be political sympathy for the
principles and objectives underlying opting-out; a suggestion that would
be supported by the negligible degree of interest in opting-out shown in
Scotland, referred to later in this chapter. However, LSI's report also
suggests another factor at play in determining the level of interest in opting-

out within an LEA area. Of the 204 secondary schools in England which voted to opt out without having been the subject of reorganization proposals under sections 12–14 of the Education Act 1980, 103 were in the lowest-spending 25 LEAs, while only 12 were in the highest-spending 25. Of these 103, 48 were in Kent and Lincolnshire, two of the three lowest-spending LEAs in England.

In Scotland, where measures closely paralleling the ERA legislation on opting-out were introduced in the Self-Governing Schools etc. (Scotland) Act 1989, no school had received self-governing status by July 1992, three years after the introduction of the Act had come into force. The only school to have reached the stage, after a parental ballot, of formally seeking GM status, had had its application turned down by the Secretary of State for Scotland, as it substantially cut across a local authority reorganization proposal (Feintuck, 1993, app. 1). By contrast, at the same time, and with the measure for England and Wales only one year older, some 200 schools had acquired GM status south of the border.

It is, of course, necessary to consider what other factors might be at play in causing such a difference in response. It should be noted that though recent education reform in Scotland has followed roughly the same broad design as that in England and Wales, certain distinctive features remain. Most notably, school boards, an approximate equivalent to governing bodies, have only been introduced relatively recently in Scotland, under the School Boards (Scotland) Act 1988. However, a further difference arises in relation to measures for parental choice of school, where as early as 1981, a strong form of parental choice, similar in appearance to that introduced south of the border only in 1988 by ERA, has been in place for some time (Adler *et al.*, 1989). In addition, the full rigours of the National Curriculum have not been introduced in Scotland; as recently as June 1993, the SOED issued guidelines on the structure and balance of the curriculum (SOED, 1993), suggesting that it was still seeking to pursue a cooperative approach with local authorities over curriculum reform, contrasting sharply with the prescriptive approach taken by central government at Westminster.

In short, a range of factors seem to be relevant to the failure of Scottish schools to be attracted by self-governing status. The relative newness of school boards, on which parents have a majority, might well suggest a reason for hesitancy, and it is clear that they have been unwilling to seek more than the basic powers granted to them (Munn, 1991). However, there seems not to have been the same degree of rapid upheaval in Scotland across the schools system as a whole, and the policy-making community, identified by McPherson and Raab (1988) appears to have enjoyed relative continuity. Finally, and perhaps most critically, the political will to make the experiment succeed, demonstrated by all four holders of the office of Secretary of State at the DFE since 1988, does not seem to be present in Scotland. The willingness of the Secretary of State for Scotland to reject the first, high-profile, bid for self-governing status, in favour of conflicting local authority plans, suggests a very different approach to his counterparts south of the border, where weakly supported opt-out bids, such as that of Stratford School in Newham, have been approved.

While such a rejection by the SOED perhaps reflects insecurity in policy deriving from the weak political mandate for Conservative policies in Scotland, the overall level of lack of activity in relation to opting-out perhaps serves to affirm the evidence from England and Wales, that opting-out is primarily attractive in Conservative controlled LEA areas, where spending on education is traditionally lowest.

It seems reasonable to conclude that Conservative control and low-spending on education are factors that go a long way towards providing some explanation of why Kent, along with authorities with similar backgrounds such as Essex and Lincolnshire, has experienced such high levels of activity in relation to opting-out.

Such evidence substantially undermines the claims made by Ministers in the early phase of opting-out that GM schools would be treated, financially, no more favourably than their LEA maintained counterparts; the claim that a 'level playing field' would be maintained. The original rhetoric stated that the purpose of opting-out was to provide parents with the opportunity to free a school from the shackles of LEA administration, leaving the school with more freedom to spend available money, and generally to manage its own affairs. It seems that it was envisaged that such an option would be particularly attractive to parents in authorities controlled by left-wing councils, though quite the reverse has happened in practice.

Though the majority of opt-outs appear to be motivated either by a perceived threat to the future of the school and/or the financial advantages of GM status, it is often difficult to identify a clear rationale, and it is not uncommon to hear that a school has opted out in order to be free of LEA influence, perhaps as a result of poor relations between the school and the authority over a long period. In such cases, it is difficult to discern exactly what the parents hope or expect to gain by such a move, if financial advantages are excluded from consideration.

Very few schools have applied formally to change their character after opting-out, and the majority of parents, teachers and governors discern little difference in educational terms arising out of the opt-out, except for better levels of resourcing. Less tangible effects, including changes of style of management, or ethos, or morale, are sometimes reported, though notoriously difficult to pin-down. Headteachers and governors do claim a greater feeling both of freedom and responsibility, though most confirm that the 'educational product' offered by the school remains unaltered. In addition, GM schools have already acquired a good deal of prestige in the eyes of parents, resulting in many being oversubscribed, and allowing those responsible at such schools a degree of discretion in the selection of pupils.

Taken as a whole, the evidence relating to the choice to opt out suggests not only that the choice is not largely that of parents, whose views are subject to significant influence by the headteacher and leading governors, and can be overridden by the Secretary of State, but also that parents are often unable to obtain sufficient information on the consequences of and agenda for opting-out to enable them to make an informed input. Ultimately, if the educational product is not substantially affected by GM status, it is difficult to see why parents would choose to take a school, if unaffected by reorganization plans, out of LEA control, were it not for the substantial allure of financial benefits.

ACCOUNTABILITY IN THE ADMINISTRATION OF SCHOOLING

Again, it is possible to use opting-out as the paradigm example of the recent reforms. The fundamental relocation of power brought about by the introduction of opting-out, notionally to parents, but more substantially away from LEAs, to the Secretary of State, to those in power at individual GM schools, and to those with influence over the sector as a whole, raises significant questions regarding the accountability of the new power holders.

Issues of accountability at each level of the administration will be considered in turn.

Secretary of State

When considering the choice to opt out, the crucial nature of discretion held by the Secretary of State became apparent. This aspect is explored more fully in the context of the litigation over the opt-out of Beechen Cliff School, considered in the next chapter. However, the degree of discretion enjoyed by the Secretary of State in relation to the GM sector is illustrated not only by specific choices between approval and rejection, but also in the ability to steer the sector, and seek to increase its rate of growth by the exercise of broader discretion granted under the ERA.

The funding arrangements for GM schools, discussed above, provide an example of how the Secretary of State can exercise significant control over the sector. At a time when the emphasis is on encouraging more schools to opt out, regulations can be passed, subject to minimal Parliamentary scrutiny, providing suitably attractive incentives for opting-out. Where natural allies of the government are adversely affected by high levels of opting-out, such as was the case in certain Conservative controlled county councils, then the power exists to amend regulations, either simply to reduce the level of top-up paid to GM schools and recouped from LEAs, or, to introduce special provisions for authorities experiencing high levels of opting-out, reducing the adverse impact of funding loss for LEAs. Equally, as implied in the 1992 White Paper (DFE, 1992) it is possible that, given the financial implications of projected large-scale opting-out, central government may adopt policies that will lead to financial incentives levelling-out, or even reducing, in the interests of limiting spending, a development predicted by Wragg (1988) following his observations of the introduction of the TVEI scheme, where early programmes received significantly higher levels of funding than those that came later.

The Secretary of State also exercises the power to approve or reject applications from GM schools for significant changes of character. Such proposals, to change the nature of a school's intake, or to significantly increase or decrease its roll, would, in the case of a LEA maintained school, be arrived at by the democratically elected local authority, and would be subject to statutory requirements of consultation under the Education Act 1980. Though Section 89 of the ERA requires publication of any proposals, and provides for a period in which objections may be lodged with the Secretary of State, the ultimate decision now rests with central government, acting in pursuit of whatever policy is currently being pursued, rather than with local representatives.

The primary mechanism of accountability relevant to central government decision making remains the parliamentary process, however, given the nature of majority government, pressures on parliamentary time, and lack of access to information for opposition groups, the efficacy of this mechanism is highly doubtful. As is demonstrated in the next chapter, the possibility of successfully using legal challenge as a secondary avenue of accountability in relation to the exercise of Ministerial discretion remains slight.

The primary mechanism of accountability present in the ERA, the introduction of market forces, fails to reach the level of central government. The potential for 'changing the management' of the country through general elections held every five years, when issues regarding education will be only one of many local, national and international considerations in the mind of the electorate, hardly acts as a severe restraint on ministers taking decisions regarding individual schools, though it is interesting to speculate as to whether Chris Patten's loss of his Bath seat in the 1992 general election resulted, at least in part, from the decision of his Cabinet colleague, John MacGregor, to approve GM status for Beechen Cliff School during his period as Secretary of State for education.

Sector level management

The potential introduction of a new range of education quangos provides a further example of education decision-makers largely free from public scrutiny and check. The problems of parliamentary control of quasi-government are well documented (Harden, 1987), and their doubtful legal standing can present difficulties in effective control through the courts. In effect, the introduction of the Education Associations (EA) and a Funding Agency for Schools (FAS), with key personnel appointed by the Secretary of State, raise the clear possibility of bodies remote from local communities managing the administration of schooling subject only to the patronage and control of the Secretary of State. Similar problems are raised by existing bodies that exercise influence at the level of the GM sector.

Within four years of opting-out starting, a body known as the Standing Advisory Committee (SAC) of GM schools had been established. Consisting of representatives of headteachers and governors of GM schools, and serviced by the GMSC, it was originally conceived, in the view of Adrian Pritchard, Director of the GMSC, to fulfil a role of advising the GMSC, and providing feedback on the services the Centre provided to schools. However, the SAC quickly took on an expanded role.

In February 1992, representatives of SAC met with the then Secretary of State, Kenneth Clarke, who, in the words of Adrian Pritchard, 'made it very clear that he saw them as the main body with which the NCC, SEAC, and the Department would liaise and consult with in relation to matters of the curriculum, and matters relating to funding, capital, SPGs, etc.' As Adrian Pritchard put it, 'In other words, the DES and Ministers see the SAC as very much a developing body with whom they will have formal liaison.' He thought that the SAC 'will certainly be a critical link on strategic issues' (Feintuck, 1993, ch. 13).

It is worthy of note that this body is scarcely ever referred to in reports of the GM movement; and thus, if visibility is an important aspect and indicator of accountability, it could be argued that this body is far from accountable. Neither Rogers' (1992) otherwise thorough review of opt-out issues, nor even as authoritative a publication as Davies and Anderson's book (1992), co-written by Lesley Anderson, Deputy Director of the GMSC, make reference to the existence of the SAC. Indeed, there is significant doubt even whether minutes of meetings of the SAC are available for public scrutiny (Feintuck, 1993).

Adrian Pritchard stressed in interviews that GM schools associated with the SAC, as with the GMSC, on a voluntary basis. Like Andrew Turner at CIE, he saw SAC as more of a lobby group for, than exercising any managerial control over, GM schools. However, he added that it was important that a body such as SAC should be available to put forward the collective view of the expanding GM sector, so as to be able to compete effectively with bodies such as AMA and ACC that represent LEA views and interests.

What the position of SAC will be in light of the reforms proposed in the 1992 White Paper is somewhat unclear, though in September 1992 Pritchard was of the opinion that the body's influence would be undiminished by the possible arrival of a Funding Agency and/or Education Associations. He has, however, expressed substantial reservations over the arrival of such bodies.

It seems interesting, and perhaps particularly revealing, that although Adrian Pritchard, in general, found market forces in the form of parental choice to be a strong and adequate mechanism of accountability for the GM sector, and did not seek wider community involvement in opt-out processes, he did indicate his concern over the fact that the proposed Funding Agency for Schools and Education Associations might not be accountable to the local community, and stated that he believed the Funding Agency should be accountable to Parliament (Feintuck, 1993). Such an inconsistency, combined with other thinly veiled concerns over the proposed introduction of these bodies on Pritchard's part, leads one to speculate, and it can be no more than that, as to why he was so concerned about the proposed arrival of these bodies.

One possible, and plausible, explanation arises from the fact that the GM sector has so far developed in a way unhindered by outside influence. Successive Secretaries of State have allowed influential bodies within the GM sector a substantial degree of autonomy. Within this space, the sector has begun to develop its own regulatory framework: bodies such as the GMSC and SAC have sought to develop guidance on the roles of headteachers and governors; have drawn up a Code of Practice for GM schools; have developed from within the movement to act as an effective voice for the movement, overseeing the interests of sector members. Though bodies such as the GMSC and SAC would undoubtedly claim to be accountable to their members, they now form the basis of what has all the makings of a self-regulatory regime subject to little effective scrutiny or influence from outside, and with the potential to serve exclusively the interests of its members.

As such, it is hardly surprising that such bodies would resist, and feel threatened by the arrival of new bodies within the sector, over which they have no control, just as the popular press, or the Stock Exchange, would prefer self-regulation to external control. Equally, a central government of a Thatcherite persuasion is threatened by non-government power blocs. It is a fundamental contradiction in a theory which advocates both a strong central state and a free market that in the interest of ensuring the former it is necessary to intervene in the 'free' market in order to avoid undesirable outcomes, such as other institutions becoming powerful. As Gamble (1989) has said, under Thatcherism, 'What has changed is the autonomy and legitimacy of most intermediate institutions. Only the central state and the institutions of market exchange are to enjoy legitimacy.'

Moran (1988) suggests, in relation to the self-regulatory structure introduced to the financial services sector under the Financial Services Act 1986, that a new 'statist' form of corporatism has been introduced to replace a previous 'societal' form. Although it might be wrong to make direct comparisons between the infant GM movement and the long-established, self-regulatory practices of the City of London, the issues raised appear remarkably similar. Perhaps the most striking similarity is in the models of regulation adopted.

Moran identifies models of regulation deriving from three ideal types: 'corporatist', 'market' and 'bureaucratic'. Just as City opinion was wholly opposed to a bureaucratic solution, in the form of direct regulation by a government department, or via an intermediary or agency akin to the Securities and Exchange Commission in the USA, so the GM movement is resistant to the imposition of new quangos to regulate directly activities within its sphere. Such a solution would in any event probably be somewhat alien to the Thatcherite brand of Conservatism.

It is perhaps superficially surprising, given the apparent centrality of its principles to so much of recent government policy, not least in education, that regulation through 'market' principles was not deemed a suitable option for either the GM sector or the City. However, such a solution was not deemed appropriate in either case, possibly, as is suggested by Moran (1988), and also by Page (1987), in relation to the financial services sector, because it did not offer a sufficient degree of stability, but also, presumably, because it did not allow the government a direct influence over the sectors.

Ultimately, it appears that, just as the government sought to produce a balance, in relation to the financial services sector, between a regime of control adequate for its purposes and a degree of self-regulation acceptable to the financial institutions, so it appears intent on doing in relation to the GM sector. In doing so, it has used in both areas a corporatist model (see Birkinshaw *et al.*, 1990) which, it is submitted, leaves relatively unchecked power in the hands of practitioners, acting in conjunction with the government, in the absence of effective mechanisms of external scrutiny or accountability. If such a phenomenon is apparent at the level of the GM sector, it is still clearer at the level of individual schools.

School-level management

Case study material reveals a pattern in which the location of power within a GM school is likely to reflect the power relationships existing within the school prior to opting-out. Thus, where a headteacher has been more concerned with overtly educational issues, and perhaps actively involved in teaching, rather than playing a dynamic and leading role in the overall management of the school, it is likely that she will continue to do so after opting-out, relying on committed and active governors to carry out many broader managerial functions. In such a situation, a broad distinction can be identified between policy management, fulfilled largely by the governing body, and executive management, largely the remit of the headteacher. On the other hand, where a headteacher has established themselves as the key figure in directing the school, and has perhaps been largely instrumental in the move to GM status, then it is likely that they will continue to play a dominant role after opt-out, with the governing body playing a passive, almost rubber-stamping role. A survey of members by AMMA in June 1991 (see Davies and Anderson, 1992, app. D), suggested that GM status 'intensifies rather than alters an existing management style'.

Equally, there is remarkable consistency among those interviewed in the course of case studies, including headteachers, governors and parents, that parents have acquired no additional role in, or influence over the management of GM schools after their opt-out (Feintuck, 1993).

While either of these situations can result in effective and efficient education for the school's pupils, equally, either may result in mis-management and/or autocratic rule by those in power. The problem, from the point of view of accountability, lies not so much in any particular power structure, but rather in the essentially hidden nature of the power relationships, and, the difficulty in identifying the focus of power, in order to render them susceptible to scrutiny and challenge.

In most cases, it seems that schools manage the transition to GM status with relative ease, and continuity of existing power relationships. However, the potential exists, as demonstrated by events at Stratford School, Newham, for things to go horribly wrong. The events at Stratford School were well chronicled in the general and specialist media throughout the first half of 1992. Quite apart from the narrowness of the parental vote in favour of opting-out, and well documented claims of irregularities in the ballot, discussed in Chapter 4 and the question of the Secretary of State's decision to approve the proposal, the problems encountered in the running of the school after acquisition of GM status raise questions of fundamental importance.

Appointed with effect from April 1991, when the school re-opened with its new GM status, new headteacher Anne Snelling found herself in charge of a school heavily depleted in terms of both pupil and teacher numbers. If these problems were not enough, her appointment itself became the subject of media comment, and she was soon to become enmeshed in the most high-profile dispute yet to hit the GM sector.

Approximately 80 per cent of the school's pupils are 'black', and many do not have English as their first language. The school routinely publishes documents in four languages in addition to English. Anne Snelling stated in an interview that though the governing body reflected the racial make-up of the local community, only two of the 24 teachers at the school in June 1991 were black. She believed that in part the opt-out fight was to ensure the continuation of a multicultural school that will serve the culturally diverse locality, though she also accepts that a whole range of different motives underlie the opt-out. Harbajhan Singh, formerly 'Outreach' teacher and leader of the opt-out campaign, was appointed as Community Links Liaison Officer. In June 1991, a 'Friends of Stratford' group was being started, but no formal Parents' Association existed, or had done when the school was under LEA control (Feintuck, 1993).

In February 1991, *Education* (15 February 1991) published a story on Stratford headlined, 'Movement's first collapse is threatened'. In it, the journal referred to the loss of pupils and teachers from Stratford School, and noted that 'The crisis is bound to provoke questions about the school's future and raise doubts about the judgement of the Minister of State, Tim Eggar', and added that Tory back-benchers had been warning of trouble in store if the opt-out was approved.

Less than a month after its first report of Stratford's difficulties, *Education* (8 March 1991) published a piece regarding Anne Snelling, suggesting that she had been highly critical of GM schools in a recent application for a headship at a Newham LEA school prior to her appointment at Stratford.

In retrospect, however, it is apparent that Anne Snelling's application to Newham was merely a sub-plot, and the general doubts over Stratford's future only a prelude, to the greatest tragi-comedy yet played on the GM stage. From February to June 1992, the leading characters, headteacher Anne Snelling, Chair of Governors Ghulam Shaida, and Teacher Governor Harbajhan Singh, became familiar names appearing regularly in the national general and specialist press.

A feud had developed between Snelling and certain governors, including Shaida and Singh, in the course of which Rev. Gerry Reilly had resigned as Chair of Governors to be replaced by Shaida. Eventually, this resulted in Snelling being suspended by the governing body on grounds of misconduct. At this stage, the then Secretary of State Clarke intervened, exercising his power to appoint two additional governors, including Eric Bolton, former Chief HMI. Allegations of racism, and various forms of sharp practice continued, and police were called to the school on more than one occasion.

By mid-February, speculation was rife that the Secretary of State would intervene dramatically, perhaps closing the school. *The Guardian* (19 February 1992) reported that Kenneth Clarke had told governors the previous month 'that he would not hesitate to withdraw funding if he deemed the situation unsuitable'. The active involvement of David Hart, General Secretary of the NAHT, on Snelling's behalf was also reported. As calls for withdrawal of the school's grant, and unruly meetings at the school, continued, an adjournment debate was held in the House of Commons (Hansard, Commons, Vol. 205, Cols. 135–43).

The three local MPs, Tony Banks (Newham, NW), Nigel Spearing (Newham, S) and Ron Leighton (Newham, NE) all asked the Minister, Tim Eggar, to respond to their requests for comment and assurances of prompt action by the government. Jack Straw, Labour's Education Spokesperson also referred to the government having been warned by the opposition, Newham councillors, and many of those connected with Stratford School, that to approve GM status for the school would lead to chaos. He asked for a team from HMI to be sent in immediately, comparing the government's failure to act in relation to Stratford GM School with their swift response to matters arising at LEA controlled Culloden School in nearby Tower Hamlets in 1991.

Tim Eggar's reply, did not suggest that urgent action was necessarily to be taken. He stated that,

> The Government intend to assist the school to get over its difficulties and to ensure that, by whatever means necessary within our powers, the school knows what is expected of it and the right atmosphere is created to allow the head and her teaching team to get on with their job. We have not hesitated and we will not hesitate to use when necessary the powers given to us by Parliament. We have made that clear to the governing body at every stage.

However, the Secretary of State was soon persuaded that positive action was necessary, and on 6 March 1991, *The Guardian* reported that Kenneth Clarke had ordered the governors to cease the disciplinary proceedings against Snelling, and ordered them to reconstitute the staffing committee. It was his view that three of the governors on the committee were, in *The Guardian*'s words, 'too involved in the row' to serve on the Committee, and that therefore the committee's decision to take action against Snelling had been fatally flawed.

By May it was becoming increasingly clear that Anne Snelling's position was secure, and Ghulam Shaida resigned as Chair of Governors, on ill-health grounds. In early June, Eric Bolton stepped down from the governing body, apparently believing that the School's crisis was all but over.

It is impossible to estimate the damage that the high-profile disputes at Stratford had on the school or its pupils. In terms of the GM sector as a whole, new proposals from the GMSF (see *TES*, 5 June 1992), suggesting the imposition of certain probationary conditions on GM school governing bodies during an initial two-year period, appear to have derived, at least in part, from the Stratford débâcle. Certainly Stratford raised a central issue in relation to opted-out schools, in asking 'Who runs GM schools?'

While the *TES* (7 February 1992) states that 'it is the seemingly all power-ful role of governors, whose powers have grown substantially as a result of Government reforms designed to reduce local authority influence, which has caused Stratford's problems', this appears to be something of a misleading oversimplification. Likewise, Ghulam Shaida's version (*TES*, 7 February 1992) appears to miss the subtleties of the situation: 'I am the employer and Mrs. Snelling is the employee. Therefore, I do not take orders from her, neither can she ban me from the school.'

What is clear from the Stratford saga is that there is no simple answer as to the location of power within GM schools. David Hart, of the NAHT, was quoted (*The Independent*, 6 February 1992) as pointing out how uncertain the boundaries are between the powers of governors and senior staff, sug-gesting however that a broad principle works well elsewhere, with governors setting the overarching policy and the headteacher as their executive arm.

Sardar Ali, a pro-Shaida governor at Stratford, stated (*TES*, 22 May 1992) that 'what the NAHT wants is for the head to become supreme in the school'. He added, 'that makes a mockery of the legislation and the rights of parents'. Shaida himself also pointed towards 'what he sees as the hypocrisy of ministers in promoting parent power and the status of gover-nors, and then interfering when they do not like what a group of Asian governors is doing' (*The Independent*, 6 February 1992).

It is difficult, however, to gain any great insight into the broad issues from the press reports of statements by those directly involved in the Stratford saga. The nature of the battle predictably resulted in sniping, and statements from entrenched positions. Indeed, the words used by Bob Balchin, Chair of the Grant Maintained Schools Foundation (GMSF) caught the characteristic mood of the participants when he said, that the Secretary of State had 'moved to tell the governing body to *lay off* Mrs. Snelling. I am sure that this will prevent then (*sic*) from *ganging up on her*.' (*The Guardian*, 6 March 1992, emphasis added). While this might illustrate the mood of the participants, it does little to explain the underlying issues. Of rather more help in this respect is Martin Rogers of LSI (*TES*, 7 February 1992).

Rogers notes the potentially 'very fragile' relationship between heads and governing bodies of GM schools, describing the arrangements as 'an autocrat's charter', and notes that the only check on any dispute between the parties is the Secretary of State. He contrasts this with the situation in an LEA maintained school, where the local authority, the headteacher's employer, could intervene to try and resolve the dispute, and could ultimately withdraw delegated powers from the governing body.

Melanie Phillips (*The Guardian*, 21 February 1992), commenting on the powers of governors and headteachers in GM schools, as revealed by the Stratford saga, notes also that, 'The problem is that the division between the two is legally incoherent and the head's actual powers therefore depend entirely on what the governors are prepared to grant her'.

As does Rogers, she goes on to state that the only person left to take control is the Secretary of State: 'In kicking out the council he has created a vacuum which has already forced him to intervene.' She concludes that, 'The law should be changed to define and restrict governors' powers. It cannot be sensible for governors to be responsible for delegating their own powers to heads.'

Though the formal answer to such questions is to point to the accountability of headteachers and governing bodies to parents at their school's AGM, the efficacy of such a mechanism, in light of the low level of attendance, and short-term interests of parents of existing pupils, is cast into significant doubt. It is worth reiterating that there is no evidence that parents exert more influence in GM schools than in LEA maintained schools.

Stratford certainly constitutes the basis for a strong argument in favour of clarifying the roles and responsibilities of headteachers and governing bodies. However, any large-scale shift in favour of power to the headteacher inevitably raises issues of accountability in the exercise of such powers, just as would unlimited power being granted to governing bodies. If the headteacher is supreme, to whom is she accountable? If the governing body is supreme, to whom are they accountable?

While it may be true that in the long-term market forces are the critical accountability mechanism, the fact is that market forces are usually the *only* external check on the operation of a GM school, and even the most ardent believer in market forces would be hard-pushed to make a case for the efficacy of such mechanisms in resolving short-term and immediately destructive problems of the kind faced by Stratford.

Though the events at Stratford School in no sense typify the pattern at GM schools as a whole, they do provide a startling example of the potential outcome of power-struggles, when informal 'accommodations' cannot be reached. It is the absence of a clear internal framework of accountability, and in the alternative any effective external check, that allowed the situation at Stratford to reach the stage where the Secretary of State was required to intervene by way of the sparingly used general powers under the 1944 Act.

In relation to the vast majority of schools, as yet not directly impacted by the effects of opting-out, a more limited relocation of power has occurred as a result of the introduction of LMS under which a significant degree of control over expenditure is delegated from the LEA to individual schools.

It should be remembered that LMS, and particularly 'formula funding', under which schools receive levels of funding directly related to the number of pupils they recruit, was introduced alongside open enrolment as a mechanism to increase accountability, and therefore educational standards, via market forces.

Though formally remaining the employer of school-based staff, the LEA has lost a wide-range of functions exercised by the LEA throughout the post-war era. Thus, the majority of management functions for each school are now exercised by the governing body and headteacher, though LEAs continue to provide a range of support services, funded from the proportion of the general schools budget they are able to retain, though the Education (Schools) Act 1992 has further limited their role by amending the arrangements for local schools inspectorates.

Despite their limited powers, LEAs retain a certain degree of oversight of the running of schools under LMS, and indeed retain reserve powers under ERA (Section 37) to suspend delegation to individual schools where evidence exists of substantial mismanagement. Though likely to be exercised only rarely, the potential power for the locally elected authority to withdraw delegated functions from a school in such a situation should act at an early stage to prevent, within LEA maintained schools, the kind of escalating dispute that occurred within the GM sector at Stratford School.

It remains the case, however, that the need for accommodations to be reached between head and governing bodies exists at LEA maintained schools under LMS, though the potential for local oversight appears a greater surety against difficulties than exists in relation to the GM sector.

However, it is true to say that the degree of influence now enjoyed by LEAs in relation to the local system of schools is only a fraction of that which existed prior to ERA. It remains the case though that the LEA retains the general responsibilities under the 1944 Act to ensure an adequate supply of suitable school places for the children of its area. In addition, the new procedures under ERA (Section 23) for dealing with individual complaints about schooling, discussed in Chapter 4, substantially involve the LEA, at least in the later stages. In pursuit of such functions, the LEA will continue to be accountable to the local electorate, both legally and through the ballot-box, and despite its relatively slight control over the day-to-day administration of schooling, is likely to appear responsible, in the eyes of the local populace, for any problems that occur. There appears therefore to be a dislocation of power and accountability; although locally managed schools will be subject in the long-term to accountability through market forces, if they fail to ride high in parental esteem, it seems likely that the LEA will retain a significant degree of responsibility for matters over which it is only able to exert marginal influence.

EDUCATIONAL PLANNING

For the moment at least, the LEA retains a general responsibility for planning and managing the schools system within a locality, though the evidence above has already indicated some of the problems that an authority will have in fulfilling these functions following the ERA reforms.

Ranson (1990a) specifically inquires into the relationship between the local *system* of schools and the effectiveness of learning produced at individual schools. He believes that arguments used by Briault and Smith (1980) demonstrate 'a sophisticated understanding of the complex interdependence of local education systems'. Ranson comments that secondary schooling is a particularly 'tightly coupled system', however, Peter Smith, General Secretary of AMMA, has been quoted as fearing that the extension of LMS to all *primary schools* would also potentially further 'fragment the system' (*TES*, 22 February 1991).

Ranson (and also by implication Smith) is suggesting that the quality of learning in any one institution is dependent upon the quality of the local education system. However, Ranson (1990a) takes this one stage further, and suggests that, 'There may now, however, be growing agreement that the quality of learning is not only influenced by the system of (educational) provision but also by the wider local political system in which it is located.' He is, perhaps surprisingly, able to cite Stuart Sexton in support of this proposition. Ranson seems to be saying that Sexton's support for direct accountability of 'producer' to 'consumer' links accountability and school effectiveness. Though Ranson would clearly not support the same, market dominated, system as Sexton, he accepts the link claimed in Sexton's approach.

Ranson appears to be searching for a model in which service users are able to influence the education service provided in schools, while the service is managed and structured in a responsive manner. In the course of this search, Ranson has arrived at what is perhaps a central issue, of how to reconcile the need to plan an education system for the community as a whole which remains sensitive to the needs and wishes of individual, or groups of, service-users.

Riley (1992) demonstrates the ways in which, under the ERA, the area of discretion available to LEAs in pursuit of such goals has been narrowed. In a situation increasingly bound by primary legislation and other mechanisms of central government control, the scope of LEA discretion in fulfilling such functions is considerably reduced.

The remarkably sanguine Audit Commission paper, 'Losing an Empire, Finding a Role' (Audit Commission, 1989) notes the move from LEA responsibility matched by power, to a situation in which the LEA must, shorn of much of its power, seek relationships with newly empowered individual schools, in an effort to exert influence over the shape of the schools system in its area. In this sense, the developments should perhaps be viewed not so much as a move from 'rowing' to 'steering', in the terms of Osborne and Gaebler (1992), but rather as a substantial reduction in the ability of LEAs to either row or steer.

An immediate and important aspect of this is the inability of LEAs, as a result of open enrolment, to manage pupil numbers, through establishing admissions limits. While this move superficially promises enhanced 'consumer' choice for parents, such a view fails to take into account the adverse impact on the community of a schools system in which popular schools are allowed to flourish, and presumably expand, while less popular schools will contract, and eventually close. It is not only that the hierarchical nature of the resulting situation poses problems for those concerned with equity in state education, but also that ultimately, especially if many schools close, the choice available to parents actually disappears, with selection being left to oversubscribed schools.

Not only does the admissions system deriving from the ERA pose problems for the community as a whole, it also creates a significant degree of uncertainty, and falsely raised expectations for individual children and their parents.

In a borough such as Hillingdon, where a majority of secondary schools have opted-out to GM status, this latter issue is highlighted most dramatically, with parents making a number of individual applications to different schools, with no degree of certainty as to where their child will eventually attend, unless, generally, they live close to their first choice school; the situation is further complicated by large numbers of extra-area admissions requests. Though LEAs are still able, generally, to find a school place somewhere for each child for whom they are responsible, the end result of being processed by the LEA 'clearing-house', for children who do not find a place via the primary allocation process of application to individual schools, results in many parents and children feeling that their expectations of choice have been falsely and cruelly raised.

Birmingham provides another example of the complexities for LEAs arising out of opting-out. Following lengthy litigation between the City Council and the Equal Opportunities Commission (*Equal Opportunities Commission v Birmingham City Council*, The Times, 27 October 1992) it was eventually determined that the local authority remained under a duty to ensure equal access to grammar school places for girls and boys, despite the fact that the vast majority of grammar school places within the city were now in the GM rather than LEA maintained sector, with the LEA therefore retaining no control over admissions to the schools.

Prior to the ERA, an LEA could intervene to protect the educational viability of schools suffering from temporarily reduced rolls, by offering additional resourcing to the school, beyond the level suggested by the school's current rolls, and, if necessary, by imposing admissions limits on popular schools, below their physical capacity, in order to ensure that less popular schools received an adequate number of pupils. While such a move may appear directly contrary to the ability of individual parents to exercise choice, it seems that the recent reforms have made few improvements in this respect, and have led to a situation in which the LEA is unable to protect schools whose rolls fall, either as a result of demographic trends, or as a result of low parental esteem.

While the bureaucratic planning model implied by the pre-1988 arrangements is clearly out of step with current central government ideology, it provided a degree of certainty, and an ability to incorporate community-wide interests into the process of allocation of school places. The present model, in practice, seems to have failed to improve the level of choice available to parents, while also undermining the ability to plan a system of schools as a whole.

It is not only the revised admissions arrangements and the consequences of formula funding that have significantly reduced the ability of LEAs to plan and manage in the interests of educational and economic efficiency, but also, again, the introduction of opting-out.

A fundamental task required of any system of educational administration is to ensure that sufficient and suitable school places are made available for an area, having regard to both quality of educational provision, and economic efficiency, or in simple terms, value for money. In pursuit of these objectives, and in response both to matters of education policy and demographic trends, LEAs have throughout the post-war period, often prompted by government Circulars, been continually reviewing the schools system, and, where necessary, reorganizing, through the extension of existing or opening of new schools, or amalgamation or closure of schools (Ranson, 1990a). Such processes have been bound by statutory requirements, most recently those of sections 12–14 of the Education Act 1980, including publication of and consultation on such proposals, and the requirement of approval by the Secretary of State for significant changes.

Since ERA, however, actual incidences of, or the potential for, schools opting-out in response to LEA reorganization plans has provided a significant disincentive for LEAs to act. Both statistical and qualitative data indicate the significant inhibiting effect on LEAs of the actuality or threat of opting-out (Feintuck, 1993). The ability of the decision of a single school seeking GM status to disrupt or entirely undermine authority-wide reorganization plans is repeatedly illustrated in case-study material, nowhere more vividly than in the case of Beechen Cliff School in Avon, discussed in detail in Chapter 4. It has resulted in a number of LEAs adopting policies of refusing to consider any further reorganization of the secondary school sector in the foreseeable future. At the same time, local authorities have become increasingly reluctant to invest in developments, such as sports facilities, on school sites, involving shared school and community use, for fear that if the school on whose site the facility is based were to opt-out, the facility, built at the community's expense, would be taken out of community control. It is in these senses that opting-out has already assumed a significance out of all proportion to the relatively few schools thus far pursuing the move.

Statistical data appear to establish beyond doubt that increasing numbers of opt-outs within a local authority area are directly co-related to both the degree of impact on the ability of the LEA to plan educational provision effectively, and, the need for LEAs to restructure their administration. (Feintuck, 1993, ch. 12). This derives not only from the more limited nature of the ability of LEAs to intervene significantly in the management of the schools system, but also, more immediately, the loss of funding available to LEAs to provide central services as a result of the loss to local authority budgets of the 15 or 16 per cent 'top-ups' to GM schools' AMGs.

LEA officers and members have repeatedly pointed towards the contrast between the quality and breadth of consultation required in the case of an LEA reorganization plan, and the often narrow and ill-informed debate occurring in the case of opt-outs, claiming that opting-out is thus fundamentally anti-democratic.

However, data does indicate that the potential for opting-out has caused LEAs to become more responsive to the needs and demands of individual schools, and indeed to maximize delegation of funding to schools in an effort to counter any financial advantages arising from opting-out. In so far as this increase in responsiveness, and in institutional autonomy, can be linked to enhanced educational provision, such a development may be considered desirable, though, no such link has yet been proven.

While the delegation of funding, and the potential for opting-out may therefore be seen as increasing the element of 'voice' available to those in power at individual institutions, as a result of the threat of 'exit' from the LEA sector, it would be surprising if equally effective mechanisms of voice could not be devised that did not carry with them the deleterious effects on planning that arise from opting-out.

Although the ERA and subsequent reforms have been informed by a belief in the efficacy of market forces to ensure efficiency in the delivery of schooling, it is also clear that the consequences of individual, atomized, choices result in a fundamental threat to the maintenance of a system of schools in any locality, or at least one that is able to produce a basically equitable distribution of a public good, immanent in our democratic and constitutional expectations.

The proposals to introduce a new range of centrally appointed quangos to fulfil planning functions hitherto exercised by locally elected LEAs demonstrates the need for markets to be managed. Even if the responsibility to row the boat has been relocated, away from local bureaucracies to semi-autonomous schools, the need to steer remains, but will in future be fulfilled by appointed bodies, accountable to and controlled by central government rather than within the supervision of a local electorate. Whether legitimacy in the exercise of strategic functions by such bodies will be ensured via suitable and effective mechanisms of accountability seems highly doubtful.

EDUCATIONAL DEVELOPMENTS

Readers will recall that the ultimate objective expressed by the proponents of ERA and subsequent reforms was the enhancement of educational standards in state schools, as a result of the introduction of mechanisms of accountability deriving from the exercise of market forces.

The absence of conceptual development in relation to educational standards in the discussions promoted by educational reformers has already been noted in Chapter 2, and as such it is difficult to make meaningful comment on the outcomes of the reforms.

Bearing this *caveat* in mind, it is nevertheless worth considering briefly such empirical evidence as yet available on two central elements of the reform programme. Both the recent report by Ofsted (Ofsted, 1993) into the educational performance of GM schools, and consideration of the performance of CTCs, suggest that these flagship projects have as yet failed to produce significant educational benefits.

Quite apart from their mould-breaking structural significance in the education system, CTCs were promoted as being schools which would act as beacons of excellence, providing examples of best practice which could be followed by other state schools. Extravagantly resourced, especially in relation to information technology, and based around active public/private sector cooperation, such schools might obviously be expected to produce exceptional academic achievements, and were certainly intended to be centres of educational innovation.

In one of the leading pieces of research into the CTC phenomenon, Edwards *et al.* (1992) suggest that although demonstrating some innovation in terms of funding and structures, pedagogical developments are less marked, and in so far as they can be identified, ironically tend to smack rather more of the 'progressive' methods espoused by the now defunct ILEA, and despised by the New Right, than of any new developments in educational practice.

While CTCs may thus have failed to fulfil their innovatory brief, it seems that the other new category of schools created by ERA, GM schools, has also as yet failed to demonstrate the efficacy of market forces in driving upwards educational standards. The summary of findings in Ofsted's report into the performance of GM schools from 1989 to 1992 (Ofsted, 1993) provides sobering reading for those who saw opting-out as a means to improve the quality of state education.

The report reveals that although GM schools have enjoyed enhanced funding

- The quality of management ranges from excellent to less than satisfactory.
- As in schools generally, mechanisms for quality control, such as performance indicators, evaluation of the teaching, staff appraisal, inspection and the monitoring of in-service training are at an early stage of development.
- Standards vary widely between schools, between subject departments in the same school and, on occasions, within departments. In this respect grant maintained schools differ little from other maintained schools.
- Examination results have improved, as in maintained schools in general, and are on a par with national figures.
- [T]he quality of teaching in grant maintained schools is not significantly better or worse than in other maintained schools.

Given the enhanced levels of funding available to GM schools, and increased freedom over expenditure, the Ofsted findings represent the very least which could be expected from the sector. Although it must be accepted that the GM movement remains in a formative stage, GM schools have apparently managed to keep up with their LEA maintained neighbours, but, have shown no evidence to suggest that additional progress, in educational terms, is being made.

Though Osborne and Gaebler (1992) talk approvingly of the educational outcomes of the introduction of charter and magnet schools in the USA it does not as yet appear that the broadly parallel developments in Britain are producing such benefits within a similar time-scale. Whether such apparent differences arise from the application of differing criteria or perceptions, or indeed whether more time will produce different reports, remains to be seen. However, it is possible that the differences arise from the particular, and narrow form of consumerism embodied in the British education reform programme when compared with the broader empowerment of service users and deliverers in the USA, illustrated by Sky (1992) and Osborne and Gaebler themselves. Whatever the nature of such differences, it is clear that localized experimentation with the form of administration of public education in the USA provides a basis for learning from, and adaptation of developments, contrasting markedly with the prescriptive and solidified re-formation of education imposed by central government in Britain.

The failure of GM schools to deliver in educational terms tends to confirm the thesis of Halpin *et al.* (1991), that the primary significance of GM schools is their place in the reform of the administrative structure rather than any educational advances.

SOME INTERIM CONCLUSIONS

The British programme of educational reform, especially when viewed with the benefit of Ofsted's report into GM schools, is suggestive of a desire, now largely achieved, to restructure the system of schooling so as to undermine the local democratic input, rather than the pursuit of identified, *bona fide*, educational ends. The ERA reforms have undoubtedly brought about substantial relocations of power, however, any linkage of this to improvements in educational standards, the ultimate justification offered for reform, appears extremely tenuous.

This is not to argue that the realignment of power within the British system of schools is not desirable, or might not produce identifiable educational gains. Rather, it is to suggest that the particular forms of accountability through choice introduced under ERA has singularly failed to fulfil its role as catalyst for educational advance. This is hardly surprising given that choice, the first element in the reform process, is clearly superficial.

In so far as choice exists for parents, and in terms both of choice of school and the choice to opt-out, it appears to be less than substantial in degree, it is often poorly informed, and in the case of opting-out influenced heavily by the opinions of headteachers and leading governors, and in practical terms is likely to be exercised predominantly by the articulate, middle-class, and assertive parents who are already relatively advantaged. This is emphasized by the still critical importance of geographical location in the allocation of school places; for those who can afford to choose to move near to a popular, 'non-selective' school, their chance of admission to their first choice school is great, as it always has been. The tendency to reproduce hierarchies of advantage is in no way diminished, and in many ways reinforced.

The choice to opt-out, which appears to have negligible, if any, educational results, is essentially a choice to receive enhanced funding. Given the enormous over-representation of grammar schools within the GM sector to date (Local Schools Information, 1992), it appears to represent further evidence of the entrenchment of hierarchy within schooling.

The result of actual or potential exercise of such atomized choice has resulted in an undermining of the ability of LEAs to plan and manage a schools system in pursuit of goals of educational and economic efficiency. The ability to direct a local schools system towards long-term aims has been removed, to be replaced by the consequences of individual choices leading to an indeterminate and unplanned result.

The proposed development of quangos to oversee the local administration of education demonstrates the acknowledgement by the government of the need for certain strategic functions to be fulfilled, though in the future by centrally appointed rather than locally elected bodies. The problems of accountability raised by the creation of such bodies mirror the issues arising out of the management of GM schools, both individually and as a sector.

Just as there exists no clear single agenda for schools opting-out of local authority control, there exists also no clear model for the management, and hence accountability in the exercise of power after opt-out. The informal and essentially hidden accommodations within GM schools raise the same problems as those arising out of the management of the sector by self-appointed and essentially closed organizations such as the SAC, while no enhanced role for parents in the management of GM schools is evidenced.

In the absence of structural clarity and certainty, and procedural openness, and in the absence of control via democratic processes, belief in the effectiveness, efficiency and fairness of power-holders becomes an act of faith. Mechanisms do not exist whereby checks can be made on the exercise of power, and power-holders called to account for, and potentially subjected to sanctions in relation to, their actions.

This chapter has raised substantial questions as to the degree to which the fundamental constitutional element, of legitimacy in the exercise of public power via accountability, is being fulfilled. Similarly, constitutional expectations of equity in the delivery of a public good such as education are thrown into serious doubt. On a broader level, the evidence suggests that the essential constitutional purpose, of guaranteeing an arena for rational discourse, is not being fulfilled. In the next chapter, the law's responses to such issues in the British context are discussed.

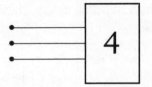

THE ROLES OF LAW IN
EDUCATION ADMINISTRATION

INTRODUCTION

In the first two chapters of this book, consideration was given to the major
themes underlying the administration of education, and the conceptual
framework within which the law operates in this area. In particular, attention was given to the relocation of power brought about by the Education
Reform Act 1988 (ERA) with the introduction of quasi-market forces into
public education in England and Wales. Brief consideration was also given
to parallel developments in other administrations, the significance of which,
particularly those developments in the USA, will become more apparent in
the course of this chapter.

Chapter 3 demonstrated the outcomes of the introduction of market
forces, focusing on the key area of opting-out, with the evidence suggesting
strongly that, while the claimed relocation of power from LEA to consumer
might be more apparent than real, a more significant and substantial transfer
has taken place from local government to central government in the guise
of the Secretary of State for Education.

In this chapter, we will return to the central themes of choice and accountability, applying the underlying theoretical concerns to the empirical data.
In particular, concentration will be on various aspects of 'legal' intervention
in the area – 'legal' being given a wide definition, as established in the first
chapter. Thus, we will consider the various roles played by the law in the

administration of public education, looking in turn at a number of different, though intimately connected issues.

First, we will consider law as a means of implementing central government policy, that is 'instrumental' use of law. It is then necessary to examine the use of law as a mechanism of accountability, for controlling the exercise of discretion both before and after decisions are taken. From there, our attention will turn to look more generally at how the law operates to resolve disputes between competing interests. The concentration in the earlier parts of the chapter will be primarily on the courts' responses to these issues, though later, the focus of attention will be on what I will call, after Ehrlich (1922), 'the living law'; the development of institutional structures and norms without formal 'legal' intervention or challenge. Finally, an attempt is made again to place the legal issues within the context of constitutional purpose. In light of comparisons with developments in the USA, issues in the administration of education will be placed in the wider context of a discussion of the roles of the legislature, executive and judiciary.

The main group of cases to be considered involves issues arising out of opting-out, the measure, it is argued, at the heart of the ERA reforms. Though the major cases in this area all throw-up issues that cut across the categorization of legal roles set-out above, they are referred to selectively, in order to illustrate particular aspects of the law's presence in education administration.

INSTRUMENTAL USES OF LAW

The use of primary legislation to revise the structure of education so as to better fit the model of society preferred by the government of the day is nothing new, and simply represents the legislative power of Parliament, as acquired by a political party with a working majority. The landmark Act of 1944 clearly fits into such a category. Indeed, the Act is often said to have reflected a broad social consensus arising out of the end of the Second World War. Similarly, the introduction of the Education Act 1976, by the Labour government, can be viewed as a direct response to the decision of the House of Lords in the Tameside case (*Secretary of State for Education and Science v Tameside MBC* [1976] 3 WLR 641), demonstrating the supremacy of the government of the day, in control of legislative power, over both political opposition and the judiciary.

However, no Act since 1944 has attempted such a fundamental reform of the education system as ERA. The Act is an unambiguous attempt to have the school system embody the market philosophy of Thatcherism. In pursuit of such aims, power is relocated from LEAs to parents, in their newly assigned role as 'consumers' of education, to those in power at individual schools, to the Secretary of State, and, following the implementation of the White Paper (DFE, 1992), to a range of new quangos.

As discussed in the previous chapter, the process of schools opting-out to GM status can be viewed as the paradigm example of the reforms, not only forming a central plank of the reforms, but also embodying the relocation of power and the theory of accountability via choice. It provides valuable examples of the legal issues raised by the reforms, and demonstrates clearly the manner in which ERA has been used to change the balance of power within the schools system, both locally, within LEA areas, and nationally.

The DES consultation paper on GM schools (DFE, 1987b) referred to opting-out as adding 'a new and powerful dimension to the ability of parents to exercise choice within the publicly provided sector of education', and stated also that 'The greater diversity which will result should enhance the prospect of improving educational standards in all schools.'

The empirical evidence already considered casts substantial doubt on the accuracy of both of these claims, in particular, questioning the centrality of the role of parents in the opt-out process.

The opt-out process established by ERA (Sections 60 to 78) appears to place parents of present pupils at a school at the heart of the process. The potential for parents to instigate the process, via a petition, and the crucial ballot process, undoubtedly suggests that the parental voice is critical to the decision of a school to opt out. In reality, however, it seems that relatively few ballots are brought about by parental petition, and that the norm is for the process to be started by resolutions of the school's existing governing body, often influenced by the headteacher and/or a small group of governors. It is clear also, that although parental opinion, as embodied by the ballot, though a step on the way to GM status, is by no means conclusive in the decision as to whether a school will opt out. Ultimately, the power rests with the Secretary of State, who may fly in the face of parental opinion as expressed in a ballot, either, as in the case of Stratford School, Newham, approving GM status where only a small number of parents have voted in favour, or, as in the case of Walsingham School, Wandsworth, rejecting an opt-out proposal where overwhelming parental support for the move has been demonstrated in the ballot.

Litigation has arisen on several occasions in relation to this power. The central cases, involving Beechen Cliff School in Avon, and Stratford School in Newham, are considered later in this Chapter, however, three other cases demonstrate the comprehensive degree of discretion successfully granted to the Secretary of State in this area.

In the unreported case of *R v Secretary of State for Wales* ex parte *Gwent County Council* (CA, 30 July 1992, Lexis), the Secretary of State had approved GM status for Cwmcarn Comprehensive School while rejecting proposals from a school in Newport. Both were subject to closure proposals from Gwent CC, arrived at after nearly three years of consideration and consultation, and both were under-subscribed and appeared to have below average academic records.

The only significant difference appeared to be that, after being provided with a copy of the LEA objections to their GM proposals by the Welsh Office, the Newport governors withdrew their support for the opt-out (*TES*, 8 June 1990), while the Cwmcarn governors were not provided with a copy of the LEA's objections.

The County Council challenged the Secretary of State's approval of the Cwmcarn opt-out on the basis that the decision must be irrational, and/or, that the same criteria had not been applied to both schools. Alternatively, the Council argued, the Secretary of State must have failed to take into account relevant factors, or, that he had acted in pursuit of some unannounced policy of preference for the principle of opting-out which he had allowed to override his duty under Section 73 to consider the opt-out and closure proposals alongside one another.

Gwent County Council pointed towards the policies on efficiency espoused by the government in 'Better Schools' (DFE, 1985), and in Welsh Office Circulars (Welsh Office, 1988a and b) that closely mirror DES guidance on the removal of surplus places and the closure of educationally unviable schools. Essentially, the Council argued that the Secretary of State would approve GM status for a school which was so small as to be neither educationally or economically viable because of parental preference for its retention, whereas he would not have regarded parental preference as a ground for retaining such an LEA maintained school.

However, Parker LJ, giving the leading judgement in the Court of Appeal, found that no such hidden policy existed, and referred to, 'the reality that there is here nothing more than a complete disagreement' between Gwent and the Secretary of State. The court cited *British Oxygen Co. Ltd v Minister of Technology* ([1970] 3 All ER 165) in support of the proposition that, in any event, the Minister was entitled to have a policy, so long as that did not turn into a refusal to listen to representations and take into account differences between cases.

While the Gwent, Avon and Newham cases all arose out of approval of GM proposals by Ministers, two cases have also resulted from the rejection of proposals. The rejection by the Secretary of State of strongly supported opt-out proposals by Walsingham Girls School, in Thatcherite Wandsworth, came hot on the heels of his approval of the equally controversial, though poorly supported, proposal by Stratford School to opt-out of left-wing Newham. Comparisons, and conclusions as to political motivation for the decision, were inevitable.

The decision of the Secretary of State to reject opt-out proposals in favour of Wandsworth's plans to close Walsingham school was challenged (*R v*

Secretary of State for Education and Science ex parte *Malik*, QB, CO/ 1241/91, 17 July 1991, Lexis) by a parent, who chose to pursue an issue that had been raised, but not addressed directly in the Beechen Cliff litigation. The applicant sought to establish that, by approval of the closure of an all girls school, combined with other decisions taken at the same time, amounted to discrimination within the terms of the Sex Discrimination Act 1975, as it resulted in an imbalance in the availability of places in single-sex places for boys and girls within the area. (On the sex discrimination point, see now *Equal Opportunities Commission v Birmingham City Council*, The Times, 27 October 1992.)

On this occasion, Rose J found that the Secretary of State had not had evidence before him sufficient to demonstrate that his decision would result in sex discrimination within the meaning of the Act, and that therefore the decision would stand.

In another case arising out of parental displeasure at a decision to reject opt-out proposals in favour of LEA reorganization plans in Dorset (*R v Secretary of State for Education* ex parte *Banham*, The Times, 27 October 1992) Macpherson J similarly dismissed the application, finding that although 'the court offers protection from abuse of power', it 'must not interfere with decisions as such made by the administration or the executive'. In case any further clarification was needed, he added that, 'it is not for the court to say whether it approves or disapproves of the decision made by the Secretary of State'.

It is clear that a range of approaches have been pursued in court in attempts to challenge the exercise of discretion under the power to approve or reject opt-outs. They have proved wholly ineffective, whether from LEAs opposing opting-out, or parents supporting purported opt-outs. Both supporters and opponents of opting-out have been consistently frustrated in their attempts to use the law to challenge the power of the Secretary of State. The possibility that this raises broader issues relating to the ability of British courts to control executive discretion is considered further, later in this chapter, and in Chapter 5.

It is therefore apparent, that the legislation has successfully granted wide-ranging discretion to the executive in relation to the approval of applications for GM status, to the extent that the appearance of centrality for 'parent power' may seem little more than a charade.

Equally, it is clear that the substantial powers transferred to those who will manage opted-out schools represents another manifestation of the relocation of power brought about by ERA. Powers over appointment of staff, and, perhaps most important, admissions and exclusions, have, in line with the government's broad strategy of reducing the influence of local government, been removed from the sphere of the LEA, and granted instead to those in power at individual institutions. The willingness of such new power-holders to exercise these powers, 'in the interests of the school', is discussed later in this chapter in the context of Queen Elizabeth School for Boys (QEB), Barnet.

The ability granted to the Secretary of State to establish, via secondary legislation, in the form of financial regulations, levels of funding for GM schools, and thus to influence the level of uptake of GM status, is also reflected in the litigation. As with challenges over the decision to approve or reject opt-out proposals, the only two local authorities so far to challenge funding decisions have failed to persuade the courts of the legal merits of their cases.

R v Department of Education and Science ex parte Dudley MBC (90 LGR 296) concerned the level of AMG provided to Old Swinford High School for Boys. The school, a boarding and day school for boys, had opted-out of its former status as a voluntary aided school maintained by Dudley MBC. As a result of its voluntary aided status, the local authority had not been responsible for structural repairs to the school, however, the AMG for 1989–90 set by the DES under the 1989 Finance Regulations included a sum of approximately £11,000 relating to such work to be paid to the school and recouped from the LEA.

The LEA challenged this apparently perverse decision, but the court found that the decision was consistent with the regulations, and, though the regulations might therefore be found to be 'unreasonable', the court quoted de Smith (1980) who states that,

> It has commonly been assumed that no criterion of reasonableness governs the validity of statutory instruments made by Ministers or Her Majesty in Council. If a statutory instrument or other departmental regulation appears to a court to be outrageous it may be held to be ultra vires, but its invalidity will probably not be attributed to unreasonableness per se.

Otton J went on also to quote Lord Greene MR in *Carltona v Commissioners of Works* ([1943] 2 All ER 560, at 564), as saying,

> All that the court can do is to see that the power . . . falls within the four corners of the powers given by the legislature and to see that the powers are exercised in good faith. Apart from that, the courts have no power at all to inquire into the reasonableness, the policy, the sense, or any other aspect of the transaction.

Otton J concluded that, though the Council's arguments were compelling 'on the merits', 'the weight of authority does not permit me to declare Regulations or the exercise of the Secretary of State's power under them perverse or unreasonable'.

A second case also concerned a 'windfall' accruing to GM schools as a result of the terms of the finance Regulations, on this occasion the 1990

Regulations. In *R v Secretary of State for Education and Science* ex parte *Birmingham City Council* (The Times, 13 May 1992) Small Heath and Baverstock GM schools in Birmingham were receiving from DES the full amount of the Uniform Business Rate chargeable against their premises, even though, as charities, they were only liable to pay 20 per cent of the rate. However, the result was again found to be consistent with a strict construction of the Regulations, and the application dismissed.

As with the cases on approval or rejection of GM status, the cases on disputes over levels of funding reveal an unwillingness or inability on the part of British courts to challenge executive power, even where it produces apparently perverse results.

Proposed transfers of powers to quangos such as the Education Associations and Funding Association for Schools under the 1993 Education Act, also demonstrate the willingness to employ legislation to further remove power from elected LEAs. However, they also raise more fundamental problems associated with accountability of quasi-government in the British context. Traditionally, the accountability of such bodies via political mechanisms, primarily ministerial responsibility, has proved problematic, given their semi-detached position in relation to government departments. Similarly, the susceptibility of such bodies to control in the courts through judicial review has been somewhat uncertain, not only because of the general vagaries of judicial review, but also because of doubts over their legal nature.

It is manifestly clear from this brief survey that the law has been used successfully to bring about and enforce the relocation of power away from LEAs, and into the hands of various bodies, but especially the Secretary of State. The statutory provisions, as interpreted by the courts, have allowed new holders of power wide-ranging discretion, which it seems may not be subject to adequate mechanisms of accountability.

LAW AS AN ACCOUNTABILITY MECHANISM

It will be recalled that in Chapter 2 it was established that susceptibility to legal challenge forms a central element of the claims of accountability, and hence legitimacy, of executive action. Discretionary powers, established by the framework provided by primary legislation, are an essential part of the administration of education. This has been the case ever since the 1944 Act established framework, rather than detailed, statutory provisions within which the Secretary of State, and primarily the LEA, would have freedom of manoeuvre. However, as part of its relocation of power, ERA has introduced a wide range of new powers, without introducing any new mechanisms of legal accountability.

Again, it is necessary to consider powers to be exercised by a range of bodies and individuals, including LEAs and individual schools, but to focus primarily upon the Secretary of State.

The exercise of discretionary powers by public bodies forms a crucial and central plank of British public law. As a rule of thumb, the court is confined in judicial review actions to considering how a decision is arrived at, rather than considering the merits of the decision *per se*, though this grossly over-simplifies the difficult task of disentangling the decision-making process from the decision itself.

The potential grounds on which a court can strike down an executive decision were recently described, as Cane (1992) notes 'somewhat imprecisely', by Lord Diplock as, 'illegality', 'procedural impropriety', and 'irrationality' (*CCSU v Minister for the Civil Service*, [1985] AC 374, at 410–11). The cases with which we are primarily concerned here revolve around the third head, 'irrationality', or as it is often referred to, 'unreasonableness'.

In Britain, the classical legal definition of an 'unreasonable' decision is that given by Lord Greene in *Associated Provincial Picture Houses v Wednesbury Corporation* ([1948] 1 KB 223), where he found that a decision could only be quashed on grounds of unreasonableness if it was 'so unreasonable that no reasonable authority could ever have come to it'.

It therefore appears from the 'Wednesbury test', that evidence would have to be produced to the effect that a decision-maker had taken leave of their senses before a court would be prepared to intervene. As Birkinshaw (1985) has written, the respect of the courts for administrative discretion 'was guaranteed by the oblique test of review . . . so that administrative laissez-faire was encouraged by the judiciary in all but the "most egregious" of abuses' (quoting de Smith 1980).

On the other hand, examples can be found where courts have been willing to find against public bodies on grounds of 'reasonableness' even where cogent reasons can be identified as underlying a decision (e.g. *Wheeler v Leicester City Council* [1985] AC 1054). It appears, therefore, that the only certainty regarding the concept of 'Wednesbury unreasonableness' is that it provides no predictable or consistently effective safeguard against irrationality in decision-making by public authorities.

As has already been observed, legal challenges in the area of education policy became increasingly common throughout the 1960s and 1970s. Examples include the courts' decisions regarding reorganizations in Enfield in 1967, referred to in Chapter 1, while the most celebrated example of judicial intervention in this field, arising out of the comprehensivization issue, is the case of *Secretary of State for Education and Science v Metro-politan Borough of Tameside* ([1976] 3 WLR 641) and it is worth briefly examining the circumstances of this case.

Though it was the Labour Party that implemented the 1944 Act in the immediate post-war years, by the late 1950s concerns over notions such as 'ability' and 'equality' which underlay the tripartite system, together with the problematically prestigious nature of grammar schools, caused the Party to substantially fall behind a policy of comprehensivization. In 1965, 1970 and 1974 Labour governments issued Circulars (e.g. Circular 10/65) seeking to persuade LEAs to move towards comprehensive secondary schooling. In 1975 Tameside MBC, a Labour controlled LEA, submitted proposals for the introduction of a comprehensive system which would have effectively abolished five grammar schools. These proposals met with the approval of the Labour Secretary of State, but, before they could be fully implemented, control of the local authority passed to the Conservatives who submitted new proposals which included retention of the grammar schools. The Secretary of State (with the power under Section 68 to give such directions as appear expedient when satisfied that an LEA, school or governing body is acting unreasonably) rejected these new proposals, and required the Authority to implement the original plan. This decision was challenged, and ultimately the House of Lords found that the Secretary of State's decision was unlawful; though the Secretary of State might believe that the second proposals were misguided, he had no grounds in law for finding them 'unreasonable'.

While the court's decision may superficially be seen as a reassertion of the LEA's right to make policy within its area, it may simply represent an example of the extreme latitude for judicial discretion allowed under the Wednesbury test. However, the impact of the case in relation to the comprehensivization issue was limited. The Education Act 1976, gave the Secretary of State the means to require LEAs to introduce comprehensive secondary schooling, but even after this Act LEA reorganizations proceeded on a piecemeal basis, and the election of a Conservative central government in 1979 effectively ended for the immediate future the possibility of a comprehensive policy being forcibly imposed from the centre.

It is necessary at this stage to return to the power granted to the Secretary of State to approve or reject applications for GM status. Having already considered some examples of responses by the courts to the exercise of executive discretion, it is now useful to consider the main, and high profile cases on this issue, involving Beechen Cliff School in Avon, and Stratford School in Newham.

Beechen Cliff School

The process which led to Beechen Cliff's opt-out can be said to have begun as far back as 1984, when Avon County Council, following widespread consultation, sought to reorganize secondary provision in Bath in order to address projected falling rolls. The authority issued notices under Section 12, Education Act 1980 proposing, *inter alia*, the closure of Beechen Cliff School.

However, in May 1986, the Secretary of State rejected the proposals. While stating that he appreciated the urgent need to respond to falling rolls, on both educational and economic grounds, 'he was not satisfied that the Authority, in planning, considering and approving the proposals, had adequately informed themselves; in particular, they had made no comprehensive assessment of the resource implications', and that therefore, 'crucial aspects of their consultation of the public were, largely in consequence of these omissions, either inadequate or misleading, to an unacceptable extent' (Letter to Avon CC from Secretary of State for Education, quoted by Hutchinson J, at first instance, transcript, p. 9).

Following this rejection, the Education Committee resolved again to review secondary provision in Bath, but postponed action until after the publication of the then forthcoming DES Circular 3/87, 'Providing for Quality' (DFE, 1987a).

The Circular, published in May 1987, stressed the need for LEAs to keep under constant review the pattern of provision and to use their powers to reorganize provision appropriately. The Circular advised LEAs to ensure educational efficiency by addressing the difficulties in delivering a wide curriculum in smaller schools, and especially smaller sixth forms, and to ensure economic efficiency, by removing surplus places, at a time when the problem of surplus capacity was likely to be exacerbated by falling rolls.

In July 1987, Avon began a new consultation process over secondary provision in Bath.

A first round of consultation was carried out in the latter part of the year, including the distribution of approximately 15,000 copies of the consultation document, and seven public meetings. In February 1988, the Education Committee met to consider the first round of consultation. In general the meeting favoured the proposal for a sixth-form college and a reduction in single-sex places. Further proposals were to be put forward along these lines, to be the subject of a second round of consultation. Again widespread circulation of the consultation document was carried out, and public meetings arranged. The Education Committee met again on 18 September to consider the results of this round of consultation, and a motion was carried, with all-party support, proposing further consultation with the governing bodies of schools to be affected by the proposals. In essence, the plan involved closing Beechen Cliff in its present form (11–18, boys) and using the site as a sixth-form college, with the city's other secondary schools becoming 11–16 schools.

After this third round of consultation, a decision was taken on 10 January 1989 to proceed with the reorganization. The plan had been supported by four of the schools concerned, but opposed by two, including Beechen Cliff. In light of the comments received, the Committee decided to revise the proposal, by extending the transitional period relating to Beechen Cliff so that all existing pupils would be allowed to complete their schooling there.

On 22 February 1989, statutory notices were published to this effect. Sixteen statutory objections were submitted, compared with almost 180 regarding the 1984 proposal. Indeed, as Hutchison J noted (*R v Secretary of State for Education and Science* ex parte *Avon CC*, 88 LGR 716), over 100 letters of support were submitted, including one from 150 parents, many of which expressed a desire that the uncertainty over the future of secondary schooling in Bath should be ended. Local primary schools unanimously supported the proposal.

In November 1988, while the LEA was engaged in its final round of consultation, the governors of Beechen Cliff School passed the crucial second resolution resulting in a parental ballot on whether or not the school should opt for GM status.

All parties at the school agree that the motivation for the governing body pursuing opting-out was exclusively a wish to save the school from closing. The Chair of the Parents' Association before and after the opt-out, has stated that a large number of staff and parents did oppose the opt-out, though she believed that no-one involved on either side of the argument really had sufficient information. She added that she was approached for information by a number of parents of pupils at primary schools, who had an interest in knowing what was going on at Beechen Cliff but who had not been consulted or adequately informed about the opt-out. Headteacher, Roy Ludlow was clear that all the efforts of the pro-opt-out campaigners had been directed at the parents of present pupils at Beechen Cliff, because, as he put it, 'you don't need to' involve other interest groups (Feintuck, 1993).

In the ballot, of a turnout of 66.8 per cent of those eligible to vote, 55.4 per cent voted in favour of opting-out, 44.6 per cent against. Ludlow put the relatively low turn-out at the ballot down to a tendency for those parents of pupils in years five and seven, who were about to leave the school, not to vote.

Following the ballot, the governors proceeded, on 17 April 1989, to publish and submit formal proposals for the acquisition of GM status. The LEA decided, with all-party support, to object to the proposal. The authority's objections pursued four issues:

1 The scheme of reorganization would be frustrated if the opt-out were approved.
2 Only just over one-third of all eligible parents had supported the move.
3 The reorganization proposal submitted would allow all current pupils to complete their schooling at Beechen Cliff.
4 That approving the opt-out would have adverse effects for all the children in other secondary schools in the city, by perpetuating the present situation.

Over one hundred other letters of objection to the opt-out proposals were received by the DES, many, like those that supported the LEA's reorganization proposals, focusing on a desire to see an end to years of uncertainty over secondary provision, and improvement in sixth-form provision.

On 17 August 1989, DES notified the LEA that the Secretary of State, then John MacGregor, had rejected their reorganization proposal, and informed the Chair of Governors at Beechen Cliff that their proposal to opt-out had been approved, subject only to a minor change in the implementation date.

The letter to Avon gave no meaningful reasons for the decision. It simply said: 'In reaching his decision, the Secretary of State concluded that the merits of the application by the governors of Beechen Cliff School for grant-maintained status outweighed those of the Authority's proposals.' There was, of course, no requirement that the Secretary of State should give reasons for the decision, however, it is clear that the contents of the previous paragraph would fail to meet any such standards which are imposed in other areas, for example those relating to land-use planning cases.

The LEA obtained leave, and issued judicial review proceedings. The measure central to the case was Section 73, ERA, and in particular subsections (4) and (5). Section 73 states that where a notice under Section 12 or 13 of the 1980 Act is before the Secretary of State at the same time as a proposal to acquire GM status,

> (4)(b) the Secretary of State shall consider both sets of proposals together but shall not determine the proposals under section 12 or 13 of that Act until he has made his determination with respect to the proposals for the acquisition of GM status.

Section 73(5) goes on to state that where GM status is granted, the Secretary of State is bound to reject the Section 12 or 13 proposals as they affect that school. Of course, in the case of Beechen Cliff, the approval of GM status for the school meant the inevitable rejection of the whole scheme of reorganization, given the school's proposed central role as a sixth-form college.

It is at worth quoting at length from the first instance judgement of Hutchison J, in light of his lucid and perceptive exposition of the central issues of the case, matters largely set aside in other judgements.

Hutchison J, in finding for the LEA, highlighted the importance of the Section 73 requirement to consider the two sets of proposals together, and stated that, in essence this requires the weighing of the proposals one against the other. Therefore, in a case such as this, the merits and demerits of the two conflicting proposals must be considered in the wider context of the whole proposed reorganization, of which Beechen Cliff School was only a part. He stated,

> It follows that among relevant considerations will be such things as the urgency of the projected reorganisation taking place; its merits and

demerits as a whole; the degree of support that it has among parents in the area; and the consequences, in terms of delay, uncertainty, and so on if it is, because of the approval of the grant-maintained status application, rejected.

Hutchison J. later concluded,

It could not . . . have been the intention of parliament to undermine such schemes by providing that a school whose future was affected by such a proposed reorganisation could effectively frustrate it provided only that it could make a good case for grant-maintained status and that that outcome was to be preferred in the interests of that school viewed in isolation (as it always would be where the authority's proposal involved closure of the school).

He went on to find that,

The Secretary of State's decision and its consequences fundamentally undermines the Authority's ability to fulfil its duty to undertake strategic planning of its education service. The Authority's proposal provides a solution for the whole area. The Secretary of State's preferred alternative leaves the area in an even more critical state.

and continued,

there was a failure at the crucial stage of weighing one proposal against another, to have any regard to the most important factor – the consequences that rejection of the Council's proposal would have in terms of disruption, delay and prolonged uncertainty for the majority of children and their parents in Bath. Put another way, there was a failure on the part of the Secretary of State, in weighing the one proposal against the other, to consider the Council's proposal for Beechen Cliff in its proper context.

He concluded that 'these linked decisions were arrived at without proper regard to the relevant considerations', and granted the relief sought, quashing the Secretary of State's decision.

The press reported Chris Saville, Director of Avon LEA as, not surprisingly, 'delighted', and referred to both the AMA and ACC as encouraged by the outcome (*TES*, 2 March 1990). However, delight and relief were short-lived. Obliged to reconsider his decision, the Secretary of State duly did so, but arrived at the same conclusion; Beechen Cliff should be allowed to opt-out, and the city-wide reorganization frustrated. The LEA again sought judicial review and on this occasion the matter was heard by the Court of Appeal (*R v Secretary of State for Education and Science* ex parte *Avon CC*, CA, The Independent, 25 May 1990, Transcript).

The Council pursued three main lines. That the Minister misapplied the statutory provisions by treating the application for GM status as paramount, that the Minister wrongly took into account the supposed existence of three possible alternative reorganization plans which supposedly remained feasible, and that the Minister failed to take into account the true extent of the likely delay and uncertainty which would be created by the rejection of the Council's proposals.

In the leading judgement, Ralph Gibson LJ rejected all three arguments, and, Nicholls LJ, concurring, said that 'it was difficult to see how the Council's challenge on the ground of "irrationality" could ever get off the ground'. He added that, 'An application to the Court for judicial review of the minister's decision was not the appropriate means by which the Council should seek to ventilate or pursue its differences of opinion with the Minister.' Certainly, the Court of Appeal's finding is much more in line with conventional approaches to this type of issue pursued by the British judiciary. Hutchison J had attempted to make a purposive construction of the statute, based on an assumption that the statute could not have intended to create a situation where an irrational decision by a Minister should override the considered and locally endorsed decision of an elected local authority. The problem is in the assumption he makes; it displays a certain naïveté in failing to note that the situation arising at Beechen Cliff was the result of a deliberate act of government in passing legislation granting wide discretionary powers to the Secretary of State allowing central government to override local decision-making processes.

The nature of judicial review, with the Courts superficially unwilling to interfere in 'policy' as opposed to procedure, and in particular the vague nature of the 'Wednesbury test' upon which the Authority's argument was in part based, conspired to allow the Court to avoid the issue as Avon saw it. The LEA was left feeling that despite having won the argument, it had lost the case. As Bob Morris, the then Education Officer of the AMA said, 'It seems the court is signalling that the minister has to act unreasonably to the point of perversity if a challenge is to succeed' (*TES*, 1 June 1990).

Stratford School

The events following Stratford's opt-out have been detailed in Chapter 3, above, but it is now necessary to consider the process which led to the acquisition of GM status by the school. Early in 1989, following widespread consultation over an eighteen-month period, Newham published and delivered to the DES, under the terms of Section 12 of the Education Act 1980, proposals for reorganization of the provision of schools within the borough. The reorganization had a number of aims, including, addressing a current surplus of secondary places in the north of the Borough, providing a much needed additional primary in the Forest Gate area, and freeing sufficient resources to allow for new secondary provision in the southern (newly redeveloped Docklands), and for the introduction of a sixth-form college.

Central to the reorganization plan was the closure of Stratford School, a somewhat under-subscribed, split-site, co-educational, comprehensive in Forest Gate with a very small sixth form. The lower school site was earmarked to be the new primary required, surplus secondary places would be taken out, and resources released to address the needs of the south of the borough.

During the period of consultation, public opinion gradually fell in behind this plan, though, not unnaturally, a number of parents of pupils at Stratford sought to stop the closure. Concerns were voiced by some Muslim parents over possible racial attacks on their children if they were forced to transfer to Plaistow, and, they expressed a general wish to maintain a truly local school.

In due course, a 'Save Stratford' campaign developed which attracted some support from teachers and governors. However, as it became increasingly clear that the Authority was not going to reverse the decision, the character of the campaign changed when it became taken over by a small minority of highly vocal governors who sought, rather than accepting defeat, to have the school 'opt-out' to grant maintained status. At this stage, support from teaching staff almost completely evaporated.

In a petition dated 12 May 1989, containing the signatures of just over the required 20 per cent of parents, the governing body was requested to ballot for grant maintained status. A photocopy of the petition was received by the LEA with a letter dated 16 June 1989, expressing the move towards GM status as being one of desperation; a last resort in the face of the closure decision.

The first ballot took place during the summer holiday. At the ballot, of the 42.9 per cent of parents who voted, 48.9 per cent (218) were in favour and 51 per cent (228) were against. Because of the low turnout (below 50 per cent), a second ballot was required and held in September. This time, of a 65.3 per cent turnout, 51.3 per cent (349) were in favour and 48.7 per cent (331) were against. This meant that the governing body, of which a large majority opposed the move to GM status, had to put forward a proposal to the DES. This task was left to the two pro-opt-out governors who had led the campaign.

In due course, a proposal was prepared, published, and sent for the consideration of the Secretary of State. Within the statutory period, both the LEA, and for the first time in any application for GM status, the governing body of the school concerned, lodged objections to the proposal.

The particular circumstances of Stratford School do not appear to be what those who drew up the legislation had envisaged as typical when devising the provisions relating to opting-out. Stratford is the first application for GM status where the move has been actively opposed by the majority of the existing governing body. This led to a decided reluctance after the second ballot to pursue the drawing up of the final opt-out proposal, a task which was left to the minority of pro-opt-out governors. The lack of active support for the proposal was undoubtedly a factor in the failure when submitting the proposals to the DES to include a full list of proposed 'first governors' of the GM school. This led to the DES requiring them to be re-published in a completed form, and a consequent delay. In addition, the first ballot had been called for at a time which meant that it had to be held during the summer holidays, clearly making large scale parent participation less likely. In light of this, the DES agreed to an extension of the time available for the first ballot.

Neither of these scenarios had been previously addressed in DES guidance, and a senior officer of the LEA characterized both of these incidents as examples of the DES 'making it up as they went along'. The same LEA officer was also concerned to point out what he saw as a blatant example of the DES being willing to ignore their own guidance. Paragraph 37 of DES Circular 10/88 states that,

> Where proposals have been published in respect of a particular school under section 12 or 13 of the 1980 Act, and the school is eligible for, and wishes to seek, grant-maintained status, the governing body of that school should aim to publish their application for grant-maintained status before the end of the two month period normally allowed for objections to LEA proposals.

As the Circular goes on to advise, this means that governors must carry out much preparatory work before the LEA proposal is formally published. In Stratford's case, there was a history of infighting within the governing body which had made progress on any controversial issues difficult, or even impossible. Indeed, in March 1989, after a number of governors meetings had been rendered inquorate by walk-outs, and after one accusation of assault, the Secretary of State intervened, at the request of the LEA, using his power under Section 99 of the 1944 Act, to order the governing body to meet and appoint required co-optees. Given this history, it was not surprising that the petition to ballot for GM status was not completed until approximately four months after publication of the reorganization proposals. The actual GM proposals were only published a further nine months later. The Authority argues that this history of internal political instability at the school was one of a number of factors militating against its approval for GM status.

With proposals relating to reorganization and GM status on the table at the same time, the Secretary of State was under a duty (ERA, Section 73(4)(b)) to consider both sets of proposals alongside each other, but to decide whether or not to approve the GM application first. On this occasion however, and following a meeting between officers of the LEA and the then Minister of State, Angela Rumbold, a decision was taken to set aside that part of the reorganization plan relating to Stratford and approve the remainder rather than wait until the GM application had been determined. The LEA was particularly pleased to have obtained approval for the sixth-form college proposal. It appears therefore that the DES was in agreement with the general thrust, and underlying educational and financial arguments, of the reorganization proposal.

However, following a reshuffle in the summer of 1990, and the arrival of Tim Eggar as the new Minister of State with responsibilities in this area, the DES announced on 9 August that the Secretary of State was 'minded to approve' the Stratford GM proposal, subject only to a change of date for its proposed implementation, a decision which, if subsequently confirmed would substantially cut across much of the planned reorganization, and indeed the DES's stated policy in Circular 3/87 of removing 60 per cent of surplus secondary places.

On 20 August, Andrew Panton, Head of Schools Division at Newham, wrote to the DES on behalf of the Chair of Governors at Stratford, enquiring as to the criteria applied by the Secretary of State in reaching his decision. In a reply dated 21 August, a DES official wrote,

> As to the criteria which prompted the Secretary of State to tell the governors that he was minded to approve the application for grant maintained status . . . I am afraid I cannot help the governors. In all such cases, the Secretary of State is made fully aware of all the arguments in favour of such a proposal, and all those against, in the terms in which they are submitted by the proposers and the objectors. He will then make his decision in the light of the conflicting views, but the relative weightings which he attaches to individual factors will clearly be subjective. The only thing I can usefully add, I think, is that he would not have considered approving the application in this case had he not thought that Stratford School would have a viable future as a grant maintained school.

The objections to the GM proposal lodged by the LEA contained apparently weighty arguments against the approval of the application. In essence there were seven key objections:

1 The difficulties which would be created in terms of ability to remove surplus places.
2 The continuing inefficiency in Stratford operating on split sites.
3 The urgent need to use the lower school site as a primary school.
4 Stratford not being viable as a GM school because of, a) lack of staff, the vast majority of whom had indicated a wish to take up the Authority's offer of redeployment, b) an extremely small sixth form, which could not compete with the new sixth-form college.
5 Lack of any commitment by the opt-out proposers to the ethos of GM

status, with the only real concern expressed being to save the school from closure.

6 Lack of parental support, as evidenced by the ballots.

7 Certain alleged irregularities in the second ballot, discussed later in this section, which if true, may have been crucial to the small majority in favour.

The governing body's objections of 21 May 1990 focused on the divisive impact of GM status for Stratford, undermining the provision of 'multiracial comprehensive education', and the ideological point that they believed that the school should remain under the locally elected control of Newham LEA. After the 'minded to approve' decision, the governors wrote again to the DES, stressing, in light of their local knowledge, the problems the school would face in terms of resignations by teaching and possibly non-teaching staff, and, the low level of parental support for the opt-out, and the likelihood of large scale transfers of pupils away from the school, particularly if substantial teacher resignations took place. Similar concerns were also voiced by other sectors of the local community, and, referring to their concerns, the governors stressed that, as far as they were aware, 'there is no significant body of informed opinion – locally or otherwise – which disagrees with this view'.

Despite a request for an explanation of how the 'minded to approve' decision was arrived at, no meaningful explanation of the process was given, but, none is required by the relevant ERA provisions. In this context, senior Officers of the Authority stress what they see as the stark contrast between the requirements of the procedures set down in Section 12 of the Education Act 1980, which the LEA was bound to follow in putting forward and publicly justifying its reorganization proposals, and the requirements made of the Secretary of State in relation to deciding on the opt-out application.

In terms of putting forward a case based on procedural defects, the most obvious point of challenge might have been the failure of the Secretary of State to consider adequately and act upon allegations of irregularities in the second ballot. LEA members and Officers are convinced that pro-opt-out campaigners, including at least one governor, visited parents of pupils and collected their ballot papers. The Authority received three letters, from a pupil, from two parents, and from a teacher at the school, confirming that this was the case. In addition, the local newspaper, the *Newham Recorder*, reported (28 August 1989) that the governor in question had admitted collecting papers, though only after envelopes were sealed and for the purpose of posting them.

When these allegations first surfaced, the DES was informed, (though the three letters were not available until later) but in a letter to the LEA dated 6 October 1989, stating that the matter had been discussed with the

Electoral Reform Society (the organizer of the ballot), and referring to the Secretary of State's power to set aside a ballot result and order a fresh ballot if it appears to him that the governing body has acted unreasonably in the exercise of any of their duties (ERA, Section 61(11)(c)), declined to order a new ballot.

What the letter from the DES official does not refer to are the alternative powers available to the Secretary of State under Section 61(11)(a and b), which empower him to declare a ballot void if it appears to him,

- that any requirements of this section have been contravened in the case of any ballot held in purported compliance with this section;
- that the arrangements for any ballot so held did not accord with any guidance given by him for the purposes of this section.

Guidance on the way in which the Secretary of State intends to exercise his powers in respect of ordering re-ballots is contained in the DES publication *School Governors: how to become a grant maintained school* (DFE, 1989b), where it is stated at paragraph 21,

> The Secretary of State has made it clear that he expects . . . any ballot on grant-maintained status or its associated procedures to be properly conducted: if this proves not to be the case, he may require the ballot to be held again.

Additionally, in a letter to all Chief Education Officers dated 13 February 1989, the DES advised that the Secretary of State,

> has powers under section 61(11) of the Education Reform Act to declare a ballot of parents void and to require a fresh ballot to be held [and] intends to use this power where he is satisfied that a ballot has not been conducted in accordance with the statutory procedures and associated guidance.

All relevant parties had therefore been given notice of the importance attached by the Secretary of State to ballot procedures and of his willingness to act in the face of any impropriety.

Section 61(2) requires a 'secret postal ballot', and the allegations of collection of ballot papers, would seem to go to the heart of the 'secret postal' principle, regardless of the absence of direct evidence of tampering with individual papers. In the circumstances of this ballot, with a majority of only 18 votes, any suspicion of 'ballot rigging' must cast substantial doubts on the validity of the outcome.

After the 'minded to approve' decision, the full evidence supporting these allegations was forwarded to the DES by the LEA, but the DES subsequently found them not appropriate grounds for a decision to require a new ballot under Section 61(11), as 'the actions complained of were not those of the governing body'. Notwithstanding the objections, and questions over the ballot, the Secretary of State ultimately decided to approve GM status for Stratford School, with effect from 1 April 1991, and communicated his decision by letter dated 22 October 1990.

Both officers and members in Newham LEA were well aware of the legal difficulties in successfully challenging such a decision. In essence, the challenge was to be based on 'irrationality'; the Authority would have to argue that this was a decision which no reasonable Secretary of State could have made.

Newham LEA faced obvious potential problems arising from the vague nature of the 'Wednesbury test'. However, the LEA also had an additional and more immediate hurdle to jump. It would be difficult to distinguish the precedent set in the 'Beechen Cliff' case, decided by the Court of Appeal only months before, in which the judges refused, in similar circumstances, to interfere with what were found to be essentially issues of political policy.

In view of these problems, it is difficult to see Newham's decision to pursue judicial review proceedings as anything other than an attempt to obtain publicity and potentially to embarrass the government; a decision informed more by political than legal or educational considerations, and which officers and members believed matched the approach of the Secretary of State in this case.

The application for leave to apply for judicial review sets out the basis of Newham's case. The Council argued that 'There is no sensible reason for allowing the school to acquire grant maintained status', in light of the factors outlined in their original seven objections set out above. More specifically, the application refers to the letter of 22 October 1990, in which the Secretary of State announced his approval for the opt-out. In it, he refers to 'the significant support of [the] local community' and the support of 'a large number of local people'. In light of the facts of this case, the LEA contended that there were no grounds upon which the Secretary of State could properly have reached such a conclusion.

The letter of 22 October 1990 from DES also referred to a judgement made in considering the opt-out proposal that, the school 'was capable of maintaining and improving its performance under new management', and this was a point addressed at the substantive hearing.

Schiemann J found (*R v Secretary of State for Education and Science* ex parte *Newham London Borough*, The Times, 11 January 1991) that the Secretary of State was able to approve an opt-out even though there was no evidence that the quality or range of teaching would improve, 'under the Education Reform Act 1988 Parliament had given the secretary of state the authority to make the decision; not the courts or the local education authority.' Andrew Panton, Head of Schools Division, Newham LEA, predictably, described himself as 'disappointed, but not surprised' at the outcome.

A further point of some interest, though probably of no direct relevance to the legal propriety of the decision made regarding Stratford, relates to the franchise for the ballot. The second ballot took place in September 1989, after the start of the Autumn term. However, the parents of new first-year pupils were not entitled to vote, by virtue of the terms of Section 61, subsections 14(b) and 15. These provisions state that those entitled to vote at a ballot will be parents of pupils registered fourteen days after the relevant governors' resolution or parents' petition to move towards GM status.

Critics of GM schools have often pointed to what they see as the undemocratic nature of a decision-making process in which the future of an entire school can be altered by the vote of only parents of present pupils of the school, or indeed, as in this case, an actual minority of such parents. However, even by the overall standards of the scheme, the denial of votes to the parents of present pupils, and indeed out of all present pupils, first years who are likely to spend the longest period at the school, seems particularly out of line with the government's claim, when introducing ERA, to be enhancing parental choice and 'consumer power', issues echoed in the cases involving Irlam and Cadishead School, and Audenshaw School, considered shortly.

Duties and discretion

The exercise of discretionary power by the Secretary of State of course extends beyond the area of GM schools. Most notably, the ability to influence the content of the National Curriculum and associated testing regimes appears to be a significant area. However, it is clear that other bodies continue to also exercise discretion in the sphere of education administration, and further illustrate potential weaknesses in the ability of British public law to act as an effective accountability mechanism.

Within the GM sector, the ability of headteachers and governors to influence admissions and exclusions policies, such as those discussed below in relation to QEB, Barnet, raises distinct causes for concern. In addition, in so far as the LEA continues to exercise power at the local level, it is worth considering the ability or willingness of the judiciary to control their powers.

Again, powers and duties of the LEA are often of a broad nature, within the traditions of British public administration. Although certain matters, such as proposals for school reorganizations and closures are subject to detailed procedural requirements under the Education Act 1980, compared above directly with the freedom of manoeuvre on opt-out approvals allocated to the Secretary of State under ERA, in other respects, they continue to operate under the broad framework put in place by the 1944 Act.

In *R v ILEA*, ex parte *Ali and Murshid* (The Independent, 15 February 1990) the issue was the failure of ILEA to provide school places for over 400 children in Tower Hamlets for varying periods sometimes in excess of a year. The claim was that the LEA was in breach of its duty under Section 8 Education Act 1944, to provide sufficient suitable school places. When the Secretary of State had been asked to intervene, he had concluded that as ILEA was, in his view, taking 'reasonable' steps to improve the situation, there were no grounds for intervention under Section 99.

On judicial review of ILEA's actions, Woolf LJ found that the duty under Section 8 was expressed in 'very broad and general terms'. He continued,

> While there are a number of standards which are required to be achieved by the LEA, the setting of those standards is, in the first instance, for the LEA alone to determine as long as those standards are not outside the tolerance provided by the section. There are going to be situations, some of which can and others which cannot reasonably be anticipated, where the education provided falls below the statutory standard and the standards which the LEA would set for itself. It is undoubtedly the position that within the area for which ILEA is responsible at the present time, the statutory standards and the standards it would set for itself are not being met, but this does not mean that ILEA are necessarily in breach of their duty under section 8.

In essence, Woolf LJ found that the duty on the LEA was in the nature of a 'target', and that failure to meet such a target would not automatically result in an LEA being found to be in breach of its duty under Section 8. It seems likely that in light of threats by some LEAs to reduce school hours for some children, as a result of financial pressures, this duty may again be litigated in the near future.

What such cases suggest is a failure of British public law to establish and enforce standards and mechanisms of accountability, both in respect to prior restraints and *ex post facto* challenges, adequate to ensure the accountability, and hence the legitimacy of those who exercise discretion in the administration of public education. The area is clearly one of competing claims, and therefore one in which dispute resolution will be required.

COMPETING CLAIMS AND DISPUTE RESOLUTION

What has gone before has raised, sometimes explicitly, sometimes implicitly, issues of competing claims in terms of decisions in the administration of schooling. At times, such disputes have taken the form of clashes between individuals or small groups, seeking to enforce their claims against wider collective interests. On other occasions the dispute has manifested itself in the form of a rearguard action by local authorities seeking to preserve their influence in the local education system in the face of increasing input from central government. Though such disputes may end up being resolved by the courts, the interests of the parties involved clearly relate more to political outcomes; where a party is dissatisfied with a decision arrived at via established 'political' decision-making process, it may have recourse to the courts as a 'surrogate political process'.

The examples of litigation regarding Beechen Cliff School and the Tameside case of 1976 both represent examples of the courts being used to resolve disputes arising out of the struggle for supremacy in local administration of schools between local and central government. However, it should not be assumed that the courts represent the sole, or even primary, mechanism for resolving disputes. In many, indeed the majority of instances of disputes over education administration, competing claims are resolved without the intervention of the judiciary, often under statutory procedures established specifically for this purpose.

One example of such procedures is the role played by local appeals committees established under the Education Act 1980 to deal with complaints regarding admissions to and exclusions of pupils from schools. Another is the procedure for dealing with complaints established by Section 23 ERA requiring LEAs to make arrangements for the consideration and disposal of complaints against the LEA or governing body of a school in relation to the exercise of their powers under ERA, and particularly, though not exclusively, in relation to delivery of the national curriculum. Section 23(2) requires that any complaint within the scope of the section must pass through the complaints procedures established before a parent can have recourse to the Secretary of State under his general powers granted by Sections 68 and 99 of the 1944 Act.

The provisions of Section 23 come into play where it is alleged that an LEA or governing body 'have acted or are proposing to act unreasonably with respect to the exercise of any power conferred or the performance of any duty imposed on them' (Section 23(1)). Though it may be that a wider range of statutory duties are covered by the Section 23 procedures, and the scope of the section has not been authoritatively defined, its main purpose is clearly to provide a local mechanism for the resolution of disputes regarding the curriculum, including religious education and worship as well as the secular curriculum, where LEAs and governing bodies are bound under Section 10 to give effect to the National Curriculum. In relation to GM schools, outside the scope of LEA influence, this duty, and the development of complaints procedures under Section 23, will be carried out only within the school.

Though Section 23 requires that every LEA shall 'make arrangements for the consideration and disposal of any complaint', which includes complaints regarding religious education and worship, such arrangements to be subject to the approval of the Secretary of State, the statute provides no requirements as to procedures to be followed. Some guidance is provided, however, in DES Circular 1/89 ('ERA 1988: Local Arrangements for the Consideration of Complaints'), which recommends that any complaint should first be the subject of informal discussion between parent and staff at school level before progressing to any formal stage.

As always, the legal position as set out in statute has to be viewed in the context of actual practice, and the National Consumer Council has undertaken a detailed empirical study of how complaints procedures under Section 23 have worked in practice in the first two years after their introduction: 'Complaints about schooling; the role of Section 23 ERA 1988' (National Consumer Council, 1992).

The report finds that in practice, a large number of LEAs had chosen to base their complaints procedures on models circulated by the Association of County Councils (ACC) and the Association of Metropolitan Authorities (AMA), and that all of the approved procedures were in three distinct stages, of increasing formality. As envisaged by the DES, the first stage was an informal approach to a teacher or the headteacher at the school concerned, followed secondly by a more formal approach to the governing body of the school, and finally by a formal complaint to the LEA. Formal complaints were consistently required to be in writing, though practice varied in relation to whether a named LEA officer was designated as being responsible for complaints.

Among the other noteworthy findings contained in the report are

- that it is generally not made explicit, and it is not necessarily implicit, that complaints from children will be entertained, and there was no evidence of attempts being made to elicit the views of the children whose education is the subject of complaint
- that there were variations in the composition of the complaints panel at both Stage 2 and 3 and that complaints panels at Stage 2 lacked independence (which would raise particular problems in relation to GM schools where Stage 3 does not exist)
- that there were variations in the time taken to investigate complaints and inform complainants of the outcome of the investigation, and also that not all LEAs gave guidance as to expected times to be taken, and that less than half of complaints at Stages 2 and 3 were disposed of within four weeks
- that only one-third of LEAs had produced a standard form for complaints (and not all of these were found to be suitable)
- that less than 100 formal complaints were received in each of 1989–90 and 1990–91, and that there is no system for recording complaints at Stage 2
- that of complaints that were determined, only a minority were upheld
- that many LEA officers and members, and school staff, had not received adequate training in relation to complaints procedures
- that there was not always adequate publicity of complaints procedures and that despite a requirement that complaints procedures are referred

to in school prospectuses, and are highlighted in the Parent's Charter, more than half the parents interviewed were unaware of the existence of the Section 23 procedure.

This catalogue of findings raises serious doubts with regard to the efficacy of Section 23 procedures in practice, and is in fact very reminiscent of the problems identified by researchers who investigated LEA admissions appeals procedures in the days before the introduction of statutory appeals committees, when great variations in procedures, degree of independence, and ease of access were identified.

The relatively small number of complaints recorded as processed under Section 23 procedures can be interpreted in a number of ways. It might suggest that there is a very small degree of parental dissatisfaction with the delivery of the curriculum by schools. On the other hand, it might be indicative of inadequate recording of complaints and difficulties in using the system, including lack of awareness of the mechanisms that exist.

The National Consumer Council report makes a series of recommendations as to how the situation could be improved. It proposes

- that all aspects of educational provision at school should be within the compass of Section 23, and if necessary the statute should be amended accordingly
- that LEAs should take steps to ensure that there is adequate publicity of complaints procedures
- that it should be made clear that complaints from children will be considered
- that various steps should be taken to improve and ensure the independence of complaints panels
- that better recording of complaints, especially at Stages 1 and 2 should be ensured
- that a programme of training should be instituted for LEA staff, governors, teachers and heads
- that time limits for the various stages of the complaints procedures should be set-out and adhered to
- that a Code of Practice should be devised relating to complaints procedures, presumably of a similar nature to that I have referred to in relation to appeals committees.

Though the implementation of these recommendations would have serious resource implications, in terms of time and money, if we are to have a model of accountability in relation to education provision based upon consumer power, then accessible and effective complaints mechanisms should be in place, and the wide variety of practice which currently exists, together with the relatively low usage of the procedures, suggests that justice is not being served by the present arrangements. 'Parent Power', at least as represented by Section 23 procedures, at present appears less than substantial, and appears heavily dependent upon the level of knowledge, assertiveness and persistence of individual parents.

It should be remembered, that having exhausted the local complaints procedures under Section 23, parents remaining dissatisfied can pursue an 'appeal' to the Secretary of State, or, if alleging 'maladministration', can ask the CLA to investigate. Though not legally enforceable, and taking rather the form of 'recommendations', ombudsmen's findings can in practice be very effective in causing LEAs to reconsider their procedures. Of course, the option also remains for suitably equipped parents to pursue the vagaries of judicial review if they believe that either the LEA or Secretary of State has failed to meet standards of legality, rationality or procedural propriety, or if procedures have been in breach of rules of natural justice.

None of this should be taken to suggest that it is inappropriate to consider the use of legalistic, or quasi-legalistic techniques to resolve disputes regarding educational issues. Rather, it is an appeal for any such devices to be sufficiently well publicised, accessible, independent and consistent, to ensure the consistent application of explicit principles. If legitimacy is to be claimed as arising out of consumer power enforced by legal devices, then consumers must be adequately informed, and procedures must be sufficiently well structured, to ensure that the provisions are applied equally and consistently in the interests of all children, rather than only those with particularly well-informed, articulate and persistent parents.

Such issues are of course equally relevant in relation to appeals against admissions and exclusions from schools, and both relate to the enforcement of claims of individual parents (on behalf of their children). Opting-out has, however, highlighted the potential for disputes characterized as competition between groups rather than individuals.

Most commonly, this will take the form of direct clashes between groups of parents concerned with a specific school, campaigning for and against a move to GM status. On occasions though, the dispute appears to take the form of competing claims of a group at a school, as opposed to a perceived interest of the wider community as a whole, typically represented by the LEA.

One of the many issues raised by the approval of GM status for Stratford school in Newham was the question of who should be eligible to vote in an opt-out ballot. The provisions contained in Section 61 have the effect of limiting the franchise to parents of pupils registered fourteen days after the second resolution of the governing body to ballot parents. This may, as in the case of Stratford School, have the effect of disenfranchising parents of new pupils at the school, while allowing parents of children still registered but about to leave (usually fifth, or upper sixth formers) to vote. This is a particular problem when the governors' resolutions are passed during the summer, and the 14-day period expires before the new intake is registered at the start of September.

Though not litigated in relation to Stratford, the inequity of the situation was referred to by LEA officers interviewed. However, argument on precisely this issue has been heard more recently in the unreported case of *R v Governing Body of Irlam and Cadishead Community High School* ex parte *Salford City Council* (CO/1919/92, 22 September 1992, Lexis), 'the Salford case'.

In the Salford case, the governors' second resolution was passed on 20 July 1992, and the electorate for the ballot therefore consisted of the parents of those pupils registered on 3 August. This excluded the September 1992 intake, which amounted, argued the City Council, to approximately 14 per cent of the pupils attending the school from the following month.

The Council argued that this disenfranchisement frustrated the purpose of the legislation, which they claimed was to maximize the parental role in the opt-out process, and was therefore contrary to the principle established in *Padfield v Ministry of Agriculture* ([1968] AC 997). In the alternative, the Council argued that disenfranchisement was 'Wednesbury unreasonable', in that it was irrational and unnecessary given the proposed timetable for opting-out. They also argued that the timetable adopted ignored guidance on timing of ballots provided by the Secretary of State which advised the avoidance of ballots that have this effect.

Rose J had little difficulty rejecting these submissions. Though stating that 'the expression of parental choice by ballot is at the heart of this part of the legislation', he found that there was nothing in either the legislation or the guidance which placed maximization of the parental electorate in a preeminent position.

That the process of opting-out, actual, purported or even possible, has an adverse impact on the ability of an LEA to plan and manage a local education system in the interests of educational and economic efficiency is indicated strongly by case study and questionnaire findings (Feintuck, 1993, chs, 5–12). LEAs were aware of the threat to them posed by opting-out from the very beginning of the scheme, and have sought, often by vigorous campaigning, to persuade schools to stay within the local authority system. When this has failed, a number of authorities, as described above, have sought, unsuccessfully, to use legal challenge as a mechanism for achieving their objective. However, at least one LEA, Tameside Metropolitan Borough Council (MBC), sought to limit the perceived damage to its ratepayers' interests via the exercise of its legal powers *before* any school had started the opt-out process.

It was apparent to Tameside council from soon after ERA's inception that one of its schools, Audenshaw High School, was likely to opt out. In order to preserve the development value of the school site, in the alleged interests of its ratepayers, the council sought to avoid the property transferring to the school if or when it acquired GM status. In order to do this, the council borrowed £575,000 and lent it to a company wholly owned by the council, which then bought the property and leased it back to the council at a rent subject to review. The intention was that if the school acquired GM status, only the council's interest in the lease would transfer. The entire scheme was implemented before the governors first resolved to ballot for GM status.

In due course, the school did seek GM status and was one of the first wave to opt-out with effect from September 1989, and the governors challenged the legality of the council's actions. The court found (*R v Tameside MBC* ex parte *Governors of Audenshaw High School* et al, The Independent 28 June 1990) that although the council had acted *bona fide* in the interests of the ratepayers, and had stayed within its powers granted by Section 111 of the Local Government Act 1972, its failure to consult with the governors of the school regarding the scheme vitiated the council's subsequent actions:

It was the council's duty to put to the governors the question, to be answered by reference to the interests to [*sic*] the pupils alone and leaving all political considerations aside, whether it would be more in the interests of the pupils to have the school buildings and grounds the property of the governors or for the school to be tied by a lease to an inimical council, and its creature company.

In many ways, this decision sits uneasily alongside the decision in the Salford case, referred to above. In the case of Audenshaw School, the interests of a small, special interest group were considered paramount, and a scheme designed to preserve the interests of the wider body of ratepayers undermined. In Salford, it was made clear that although the legislative intent seemed to demand the maximization of parental involvement, a procedure which disenfranchised a significant number of parents, surely part of an identifiable 'special interest group', was acceptable.

The divisive potential of opting-out relates not only to the opt-out process, but also, at least potentially, to the role of GM schools within the community. There is little doubt that, either overtly or covertly, many GM schools are already becoming essentially selective in terms of intake. This may take the form of selecting those children most academically able, who are therefore most likely to contribute to the performance of the school as reflected in league tables of exam results, and such a step is likely to reinforce existing societal inequalities that manifest themselves in 'academic ability'. In addition, without the protection against racial segregation provided in the USA in relation to charter and magnet schools, the potential for selection leading to 'all-white' GM schools is very real. Selection by reference to criteria applied at schools such as QEB, Barnet, such as the ability of potential pupils and parents to play a full role in the whole life of the school, or by reference to the maintenance of the ethos of a school, can easily take the form of racial or cultural exclusivity.

Emphasis on the 'right children and right parents' appears to offer significant potential for a school, if oversubscribed, to recruit 'in its own image'. Combined with an exodus of teachers opposed to GM status, the potential for the school to become rather homogeneous, or exclusive, appears substantial, and, reports during the summer of 1992 suggested that QEB may have been moving still further in this direction. In July 1992 it was reported (*The Independent on Sunday*, 26 July 1992) that more than 12 parents had withdrawn their sons from the school after pressure amounting to threats that if the boys were not withdrawn they would be expelled as a consequence of relatively minor alleged disciplinary offences. Though headteacher Eamonn Harris was reported as rejecting such accusations as 'offensive and untrue', a further report (*TES*, 3 July 1992) claimed that governors at another Barnet school had said in a letter that GM status meant that schools could 'refuse entry to troublemakers' and that some schools in Barnet already used a high rate of expulsion to 'select the pupils they wish to educate'.

Barnet LEA, despite having no control over QEB, was reported (*The Guardian*, 4 August 1992) as having asked the Secretary of State to investigate allegations which amounted to claims that the school had pursued a 'campaign to shed problem pupils and those under-achieving'. Though Eamonn Harris was reported as denying forcing parents to withdraw children, *The Guardian* (4 August 1992) was able to quote him as saying that, 'A value system is to the fore in Queen Elizabeth school education. It is expected that that value system is shared by the parents.' The report went on to note that, 'Parents testify to the rigour with which they are interviewed before their sons go to the school. If they do not seem to share the school's value system, Harris says he "tries very hard to persuade them to send their sons elsewhere".'

Edwards and Whitty (1992) note an interesting irony that, while open enrolment and the Greenwich ruling have the consequence of allowing oversubscribed schools to recruit, and potentially 'cream off' quality students from a wide surrounding area, specific conditions are imposed on CTCs to ensure that they must recruit from an immediate locality, and must recruit pupils of a representative ability range.

THE LIVING LAW

As the above examples demonstrate, it is important to remain aware that a study of the statutes and cases will reveal only a partial picture of the arrangements for education administration; though the only group directly involved in the opt-out process by virtue of the statutory arrangements are parents of present pupils, it is clear that it is possible, though by no means inevitable, that groups outside the school may be able to influence events. Equally, parties within the school, such as headteachers, other teachers and governors are likely to have a significant influence over parental opinion. Thus, especially in relation to new or recent developments such as opting-out, it is necessary to look beyond the 'black-letter law', and to consider tangible manifestations of newly established power relationships; the evidence presented in Chapter 3 suggests the crucial importance of such relationships. The GM sector again provides valuable examples of how informal relationships may operate within the legal framework to influence critically the management of schools.

One obvious example is the way in which admissions to and exclusions from GM schools are managed. Though the admissions arrangements for a GM school will have been approved by the Secretary of State as part of the Articles of Government, it is clear that a significant amount of discretion remains available for those who administer the arrangements. Though such arrangements will often include, for 'non-selective' schools, proximity and attendance of siblings at the school, and possibly priority for children with special educational or medical needs for whom the school is equipped to deal, other factors may be rather more subjective. For example, it is possible for admissions criteria to include factors such as willingness or otherwise of the child and/or parents to support and take part in extra-curricular activities, often outside of school hours, such as sport, music and drama. The senior teacher at one school stressed that the intention was to admit the 'right children and right parents'. While it may be perfectly understandable that a school would seek to admit children who fit the ethos of the school, the application of such criteria clearly indicates the potential for the creation of homogeneous and exclusive schools, in which choice has been transferred from its notional location with parents, to those who administer the school.

It is also clear that within the GM sector, the power relationships within the school will be crucial to the running of schools. The location of power is not established by the statute, and has not yet been the subject of litigation, despite having been given a high profile by the feud at Stratford School, Newham, described in Chapter 3.

The crucial nexus of power lies between the headteacher and governors, and, generally, it seems that the balance of power is likely to reflect the relationship existing prior to opting-out. Thus, where a headteacher or senior governor was powerful before, they are likely to be so after opt-out. If anything, with the removal of the external influence of the LEA, it seems probable that such relationships may be somewhat heightened or exaggerated following opt-out. However, where such an informal accommodation cannot be reached, a very real potential exists for the kind of destructive battle experienced at Stratford, ultimately ended in that case by the intervention of the Secretary of State.

The problem with the dependency on this process of informal accommodation is primarily that the process is hidden and inexplicit, rather than open to scrutiny either by those with an immediate involvement with the school, or for the public as a whole. The public lawyer is concerned not only with the exercise of discretionary powers such as those applied by headteachers or the Secretary of State, but also with how power is allocated, and is likely to be alarmed by the existence of essentially hidden and corporatist arrangements. In terms of the avowed intention of education legislators in recent times, to increase the power of parents in matters of schooling, the potential for corporatist arrangements to exclude the very interest group said to be empowered seems somewhat anomalous.

The corporatist tendency within the institutional structure is apparent not only at individual GM schools, but also at the level of the sector as a whole, in the important SAC, discussed in Chapter 3, where corporatism is the all pervasive model.

ADMINISTRATION AND THE CONSTITUTION

If we return now to the essential constitutional purpose identified in Chapter 1, it becomes clear that in many respects the existing administrative law framework for education in Britain, both as manifested in statute and case law, and in its living law forms, fails to fulfil the purpose of establishing and maintaining a forum in which meaningful discourse is ensured.

The narrow and often ill-informed nature of debate on opting-out, the prescriptive approach to the National Curriculum by central government, and the corporatist tendencies in administrative structures all suggest a system which fails to ensure a wide-ranging, well-informed and participative process of decision-making in the administration of schooling. It seems that appropriate mechanisms of accountability have not been introduced alongside new developments.

The responses of British courts when faced with issues in this area serve to accentuate such failings. Faced with situations in which the application of primary and/or secondary legislation, or other administrative action produces patently irrational outcomes, especially in terms of preserving a collective interest in equity in education, the courts have been unwilling or unable to provide answers that support this fundamental constitutional and democratic aim. In the absence of clear constitutional principles, the courts have applied case law on an *ad hoc* basis, and have, whether they like it or not, felt forced to accept that within the British system, the courts have no power to challenge primary legislation, even in an era in which membership of the

EC is said to have involved a derogation from the supremacy of Parliament. The cases suggest also that British courts often fail even to act as an effective avenue of challenge to secondary legislation and executive action. Thus, those excluded from initial decision-making processes may also be denied an effective mechanism of challenge after decisions have been taken.

As Hinds (1991) demonstrates, British courts can on occasion act effectively to support requirements of consultation arising out of the decision-making process. Examples from the field of education administration include *R v Brent LBC* ex parte *Gunning* ([1967] 84 LGR 168) in which the court found a 'legitimate expectation' of consultation, despite the absence of a statutory right; and *Bradbury v Enfield LBC* ([1967] 3 All ER 434) where the Court of Appeal intervened to ensure that an LEA complied with statutory requirements to give notice of an intention to implement school reorganization plans. As Danckwerts LJ observed in the latter case, 'In cases of this kind it is imperative that the procedure laid down in the relevant statutes should be observed. The provisions of the statutes in this respect are supposed to provide safeguards for Her Majesty's subjects.' This, however, demonstrates only a willingness on the part of the courts to intervene on occasion, usually when a clear, statutory, procedural requirement has been broken, and even here, recent judgements demonstrate that its circumstances may lead a court to conclude that consultation requirements may not in fact be mandatory. It is not always the case that statutes granting discretionary power place such procedural demands upon decision makers, or indeed that such procedural requirements as are imposed are effective in ensuring consistency and equity, and high quality decision making, as is demonstrated by the cases on approval of GM status discussed above. In the absence of such specific requirements, or in the presence of only ineffective statutory safeguards, British courts often seem powerless to effect control over the decision-making process in the absence of over-arching constitutional principles of procedural propriety.

It is perhaps instructive to consider the approach found in the USA where, albeit in a very different constitutional context, the courts have been instrumental in establishing and ensuring administrative processes that go some way towards avoiding such problems. Jung and Kirp (1984) note how a concept of civil rights has informed the debate on administration of schooling in the USA throughout the twentieth century. This has manifested itself not only in high profile attempts to address racial segregation by measures such as 'bussing', but also in a process which they describe as 'legalization' within schools.

Kirp (1976) describes the impact of the development of due process hearings within the school for dealing with issues such as exclusions. Due process within the context of US schools has often taken the form of formal adversarial hearings, akin to the formal procedures of the court room. There is, of course, some danger that the introduction of such processes will produce little in the way of substantive change, and may ultimately become little more than tokenism. However, both within the school setting, and more generally, Kirp notes that the utilization of a tripartite dispute resolution model, embodying due process requirements, for the resolution of bipartite disputes, feeds into essential constitutional aims, in that it 'commands rational inquiry into the circumstances of a particular dispute prior to any attempt at unilateral resolution' (Kirp 1976, p. 847).

While this is a relatively uncontroversial proposition at the level of disputes primarily concerning individuals, such as cases of exclusion of a child from school, the nature of the process may not necessarily prove as effective in dealing with collective claims, or matters deriving from broader arguments over social equity. As Kirp himself observes, there exists a substantial danger that procedural solutions may be perceived 'as resolving, rather than ameliorating, profound societal dilemmas'. He notes that to equate fair outcomes with civilized means of reaching outcomes can be 'profoundly, even tragically, mistaken' (Kirp, 1976, p. 876).

As Osborne and Gaebler (1992) and Sky (1992) indicate, since 1989, the agenda in USA education administration has increasingly focused around a theme of choice, familiar in Britain, and one that savours greatly of equity. Whether such developments do ultimately contribute to greater equity in the distribution of educational resources, or in educational outcomes, remains to be seen, however, it is inevitable, as already seen in the British context, that some disputes will ultimately appear before the courts for resolution, and it then becomes crucial to examine how far the mechanisms available to the courts will enable them to bring about resolutions that serve constitutional goals.

In the USA, not only are the courts able to construe primary legislation with reference to constitutional principles, and to enforce requirements of openness under the Administrative Procedures Act, Freedom of Information Act and government 'in the sunshine' legislation, but also, the requirements of due process in administrative action have also been bolstered by the development and enforcement by the courts of techniques such as 'hybrid rule making', and the 'hard look doctrine', requiring decision-makers to pursue processes appropriate to the situation, ranging from bare notice and comment requirements to full-scale public inquiries, and to demonstrate that all available options have been fully considered and evaluated (Stewart 1975 and Harden and Lewis, 1986). The enforcement of such requirements requires decision makers, if challenged, to produce a full 'record', which can be considered by the court, and, if indicative of failures on the part of decision-makers, can lead to judicial striking-down. Despite the potentially retrograde implications of *Vermont Yankee*, Longley (1990 and 1993) demonstrates how the existence of such requirements can have a significant influence on the shaping of policy, and substantive outcomes, in the area of public health care, an area in which recent reforms in Britain have closely paralleled those in education. As Kahn-Freund (1974) warns, however, it is necessary to consider differences in socio-political and cultural background before attempting legal transplants from one jurisdiction to another.

The absence in the UK of such judicially developed techniques as can be seen in the USA, reflecting and giving life to fundamental constitutional principles and goals, in many ways reflects the less buoyant position within the constitutional settlement enjoyed by British judges when compared with their counterparts across the Atlantic. The more dominant position of the American judiciary, reflected in greater judicial activism, contrasts markedly with the defensive and unprincipled development of administrative law in Britain, where the focus of public law discourse is essentially case rather than principle oriented. It tends to confirm that the development of a coherent and effective system of public law depends crucially upon the relationship between the legislature, executive and the judiciary, and stresses the importance of viewing the processes of administrative law, as they impact on an area such as schooling, within a broader constitutional context.

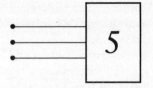

CONCLUSIONS

THE GOALS OF EDUCATIONAL REFORM

In the first two chapters of this book the goals of the state school system were defined in terms of developing children's abilities both for the benefit of the individual child and for the benefit of the community in which they live. This duality of purpose reflects the dual nature of citizenship, in which individual rights as a citizen run alongside the right to participate in the political community. Thus, education, and citizenship both include individualistic and collective elements.

The agenda for educational reform pursued by the recent Conservative governments in Britain has had at its head the improvement of educational standards, a goal which, if considered uncritically, should feed into both aspects of the education enterprise. However, to accept this aim as a clear and achievable objective is to fail to consider the complexity, and to ignore the wholly undeveloped nature of the concept of educational standards as employed in the rhetoric of recent legislators. Leaving on one side for the moment the problems of defining standards, and establishing objectives for the school system, it is necessary again to consider the mechanisms by which improvements are said to be being brought about.

The government's reforms have contained two main, potentially conflicting, thrusts. First, the establishment of a national curriculum, establishing a core of 'knowledge' which must be 'delivered' to all children in state schools, the only exceptions being CTCs, and children with identified special educational needs who may be excluded. This in itself raises difficult questions regarding the determination of the content and structure of schooling, and also acts as a limit on meaningful parental choice. Given that the quantity of material and testing required under the National Curriculum has left teachers with little time or energy for going beyond the prescribed material, the vast majority of schools will be able to offer little variety in terms of content, with choice between schools, such as it is, therefore being limited to issues such as style of teaching and management, and the ethos and prestige of the school, together with a school's ability to deliver on non-mainstream activities such as sports, music, and so on.

However, the primary focus of this book has been on the second major aspect of recent reforms, in which choice and competition have been introduced into the state school system. The justification offered for the replacement of a system in which the democratically elected LEA was the dominant party in the planning and management of a local system of schools by a system driven principally by market forces (with money following pupils, making them the primary unit of resource) has been that the exercise of parental choice would act to enhance the accountability of those exercising power over schooling; those schools that did not pay heed to consumer choice and deliver a product attractive to consumers would lose their market share, and would potentially be subjected to the ultimate market sanction of closure.

One aspect of this is to an extent being borne out, as it is obvious that some parents will seek, if reasonably practicable, to move their children from schools they do not like to those schools they prefer, thus threatening the future educational and economic viability of the schools that suffer declining resources. There is, however, no reason to suppose, and no evidence to suggest, that this has or will lead unpopular schools to improve their educational standards. Indeed, it hardly seems likely that a school's performance will improve as its resources decrease.

The scheme of reform has, however, not only been presented as a mechanism for improving educational standards, but has also been located within the broad programme of Thatcherism, and, more recently, that of Prime Minister Major.

EDUCATION REFORM AND CITIZENSHIP

The ERA, and subsequent reforms of schooling, reflect clearly the Thatcherite agenda identified by Gamble (1989), of government via market forces and a strong central state, with no significant intermediate or alternative power blocs. The remodelling of the state results in a far-reaching withdrawal of the state from the role of provider, to one in which at most it acts as a facilitator for the provision of 'public' services; in Osborne and Gaebler's terms, a move from 'rowing' to 'steering'.

The centrality of choice for individuals, as the only legitimate societal unit, within this programme has now been reinforced under the Major government by general, high-profile initiatives such as the Citizen's Charter, and with education specific measures such as the Parent's Charter, given legal form in the Education (Schools) Act 1992.

The particular concept of 'citizenship' employed in such developments is not one that fits with the dual nature of citizenship identified earlier. Though the introduction of substantive rights appears to support the individualistic aspects of citizenship, even here the practical significance of rights such as choice of school is thrown into question by empirical evidence, and the nature of decision-making processes in the post-ERA period suggest strongly that the second aspect of citizenship, that of active participation in a political community, has not even been paid lip-service, let alone positively considered or strengthened.

Though the delegation of functions to individual schools *may* produce educational benefits, and the introduction of new substantive rights for individual parents *may* enhance their role as citizens, the process of atomization inherent in the reforms appears to have had a wholly deleterious effect on the important collective aspects of the broader notion of citizenship.

THE OUTCOMES OF REFORM

A problem arises when attempting to assess the outcomes of recent reform as a result of the undeveloped concept of educational standards. Given that the ultimate objective of the reforms was said to be the improvement of standards in schools, it remains necessary to attempt to assess whether the measures introduced have yet had any positive outcomes in this respect.

Even though it seems likely that the full effect of such major reform will take some time to filter through, the government has as yet produced no convincing evidence indicating that the national curriculum and its associated testing arrangements have produced any identifiable improvements. Similarly, research carried out by Ofsted (1993) indicates that GM schools, now clearly a central pillar of the reform programme and a concrete manifestation, claims the government, of the exercise of parent power, have performed no better than their LEA maintained counterparts, despite the financial advantages attaching to opting-out. In many respects, however, parental choice has been presented not only as a means to drive-up educational standards, but also as an end, or a 'good' in itself.

The real degree of choice available to parents is, however, rather less than it might superficially appear. The presence of the National Curriculum severely limits the amount of choice available to parents in terms of educational content, while the predictable oversubscription enjoyed by popular schools, means that it is probably still more sensible to think in terms of a right to express a preference as to a school, rather than a right to choose, given that ability to obtain a place at a popular school is still likely to depend on the ability of parents to live, and if necessary to move to live, close to that school, since proximity remains a key criteria in the allocation of places in most 'non-selective' schools.

The unequal level of choice available to different groups of parents must also be considered more generally. As Ranson (1988) has put it:

> Within the marketplace all are free and equal, only differentiated by their capacity to calculate their self-interest. Yet, of course, the market masks its social bias. It elides, but reproduces, the inequalities which consumers bring to the marketplace. Under the guise of neutrality, the institution of the market actively confirms and reinforces the pre-existing social order of wealth and privilege.

The very real potential for schools to select students, overtly or covertly, by reference to academic ability, or by their ability to fit the ethos of a school, and the issues raised by this phenomenon has already been indicated at Chapters 3 and 4.

Even in the supposedly parent-centred process of opting-out, evidence suggests significant doubts as to the quality of information and debate available to parents, and demonstrates that headteachers and influential governors may have at least as important a role to play in the process as do parents of present pupils. More generally, the introduction of competition into the state school system has produced a series of important consequences, not necessarily apparent from the rhetoric associated with the reforms.

It is clear that where schools have to compete for the basic unit of resource – that is, pupils – some schools will be more successful than others. Thus, popular schools will attract large numbers of pupils and will therefore receive proportionately higher levels of funding, enabling them to preserve or enhance their popularity. Equally, it may enable schools to select, openly or not, pupils that will perform well against criteria such as examination league tables, thereby further bolstering the school's position in the marketplace. Such schools will either expand, presumably leading to the closure of other local schools, or will become increasingly selective. In either case, the result seems likely to be a reduction in choice for parents.

Meanwhile, less popular schools will inevitably attract fewer pupils and therefore proportionately less funding, and will certainly not be able to select pupils. Such schools, with more limited resources, may therefore be unable to enhance or even maintain their position in parental esteem, will therefore attract fewer pupils, receive less funding, and enter an apparently inescapable spiral of decline. It needs to be emphasized that the slow demise of a school increasingly starved of resources is not just a problem for the school as an institutional entity, or for its staff, but will have immediate damaging effects on the children unfortunate enough to attend it.

Both Lewis (1993b) and Osborne and Gaebler (1992) emphasize their belief in, and belief that government should be informed by, a concept of 'equity'. It is not apparent how a hierarchy of schools, whether introduced or simply accentuated by the recent reforms, can serve this end. Indeed, it seems that, like the other collective values inherent in citizenship, equity has also not been enhanced, and in practice appears to have been positively diminished, by the introduction of market forces into schooling.

The claim that the reforms would lead to enhanced accountability in education decision making also appears not to be borne out by empirical evidence. Within the area of opting-out, it is apparent that both at the level of individual schools and at the level of management of the GM sector there exists significant potential for power to be exercised in an essentially corporatist and hidden manner. The ability of parents to influence the management of a GM school is no greater than under LEA control, and indeed, without the external influence of the LEA it is possible for headteachers or governors to carve-up and exercise power subject to minimal public scrutiny. Likewise, bodies such as the GMSC and SAC of GM schools are able to exert considerable influence over the direction of the sector, and have direct input into central government decision-making processes, while being themselves subject to little or no external influence or scrutiny.

In the particular form of corporatism apparent in the new schools system, those most immediately concerned with the management of state education, the teachers who work in schools, and most parents, are excluded from meaningful influence. In a process of reification, power is said to have been transferred to 'the school', mystifying and masking a very real transfer of wide-ranging discretion to individual power-holders in the form of headteachers and governors, and to central government.

Ultimately, it has to be concluded that the measures relating to opting-out and the management of the GM sector have resulted in no significant enhancement in parental influence over schools, and, by removing the potential for influence by the democratically elected LEA, without the introduction of any new or additional mechanisms of scrutiny, have substantially increased the potential for autocracy and arbitrariness within the administration of state schools. In failing to ensure a role for the citizenry, both as individuals and as a collective entity, the measures fail to deliver not only the promises contained in the rhetoric of the reformers, but also the broader constitutional promise of meaningful discourse.

Perhaps of even more immediate concern is the impact that open enrolment, local management of schools (LMS) and opting-out have had on the ability to maintain and develop a system of schools within a locality.

All of these developments have contributed to an increasing inability on the part of LEAs, or any other body, to plan and manage local schools, as a system, in the interests of economic and educational efficiency, and in the maintenance of a system, as opposed to a random assortment, of schools. The most obvious symptom of these developments is the confusion over admissions to schools, especially in areas where high levels of opting-out have taken place. However, actual or potential opting-out also acts as a significant disincentive for LEAs to reorganize schooling provision in the interests of educational or economic efficiency. A proposal to amalgamate or close schools, is very likely to spark opt-out bids, while local authorities are increasingly unwilling to risk major investment in school premises, especially in facilities designed to be used by both the school and the wider community, when the potential exists for schools to opt-out, taking such assets out of local authority control.

The fact that such planning problems exist is confirmed by the 1993 Education Act measures introducing quangos such as Education Associations and the Funding Agency for Schools. Such developments confirm the need for planning and management in the schools system, but in themselves throw up new problems of how these, central government appointed, bodies will be rendered accountable in the exercise of their powers, highlighting again the fact that new and appropriate mechanisms of accountability, appropriate to new institutional designs, have not been devised and introduced.

Osborne and Gaebler (1992) note, with apparent enthusiasm, the implementation of the ERA reforms, and specifically opting-out, in Britain. In view of the outcomes of reform identified above, their enthusiasm for such developments, as examples of 'entrepreneurial government', is perhaps surprising given their avowed belief in equity and in 'ownership' of public services by users and deliverers.

The very real tensions between diversity and equity have neither been addressed nor resolved; as Codd (1991) notes in relation to developments in education in New Zealand, 'The assumption that equity can be achieved by increasing individual choice is central' to the education reform programme undertaken there. He goes on to note that 'This "free market" ideology readily coheres with popular common sense beliefs about government interference in the lives of individuals', and that 'It can become, therefore, a powerful source of legitimation.'

For avowed supporters of equity, such as Osborne and Gaebler (1992), to favour recent reforms of state education systems may appear illogical in light of the evidence presented on the reforms in Britain. However, such an apparent inconsistency diminishes if their comments are viewed in their context as being written in the USA, where, as Osborne and Gaebler themselves amply illustrate, and as confirmed by Parker (1993) and Sky (1992), such reforms form only one element of a wide range of experimentation in new governmental forms, including the active involvement of teachers in the administration of education, and where the introduction of choice is tempered by the requirement to work within wider social programmes such as those aimed at desegregation. The absence of such 'systemic controls' (Edwards and Whitty, 1992) overseeing and limiting the exercise of market forces in British schooling is in marked contrast with developments described in the USA.

As Osborne and Gaebler (1992, p. 102) note:

> Even public choice systems must be carefully structured to ensure equity, of course. Parents need reliable information about the quality of each school, and particular efforts must be made to get that information to low-income, poorly educated parents. Students need free transportation. Integration must be preserved – something many districts do by setting a bottom line for the percentage of minority students in each school.

The evidence presented in this book has indicated how those who have introduced market principles into British schooling have singularly failed to ensure that such requirements are met.

In Britain, the implications of the introduction of market forces are already becoming clear. Notions of equity and active citizenship have not been enhanced, or indeed have been diminished; choice is largely tokenistic, but where it can be exercised effectively, is likely to be utilized only by those already relatively advantaged in the distribution of resources, serving to entrench hierarchy within the state school system. Meanwhile, the new power structures introduced have failed to bring with them mechanisms adequate to ensure accountability and non-arbitrariness. The essential collective elements of citizenship have been seriously, perhaps fatally, attacked, and the constitutionally central structure of an arena for rational discourse has been fundamentally breached.

What has been provided instead is a series of substantive rights, such as choice of schools, and rights to information, which on closer inspection prove to be more apparent than real. The essentially tokenistic nature of these rights serves to confirm the belief expressed by the Director of Choice in Education, the pro-opting-out group, when he described parents merely as 'a means of legitimizing a change' (Feintuck, 1993, p. 368).

A HARD LOOK, OR JUST HARD LUCK?

The failure of the British legal system either to breathe life into the notional rights created by ERA, or to ensure that those granted powers are held accountable, is apparent from the cases considered in the previous chapter.

It is of course true to say that within the constitutional structure of Britain, the courts are deemed not to have the power to review legislative acts, provided only that Parliamentary procedures have been duly followed. As Harden and Lewis (1986) have observed, the supremacy of the legislature, 'Parliamentary omnicompetence', has been replaced in modern times, with the coming of a strong party political system, and, given generally adequate government majorities, with a new reality of executive omnicompetence. The tenuous nature of Parliament's control over the government was illustrated vividly in the summer of 1993 by the government's apparent intention to proceed with the ratification of the Maastricht Treaty, without the Social Chapter, even if necessary in the face of the expressed 'will' of the Commons.

In such a situation, where parliamentary procedures do not readily make for effective scrutiny or checks on government power, the potential for the judiciary to act as an external check becomes of crucial importance. A defensive or ineffective judiciary, that fails to rise to such a challenge, does a great disservice to the constitution.

It is not only as a result of the courts' acceptance of a constitutionally subservient position that such rights remain tokenistic, but also as a result of the absence of clear constitutional principles to which the courts can have resort. Thus, as is demonstrated in Chapter 4 the court may only have recourse to an *ad hoc* assembly of case law, deriving as much from common law as public law foundations, rather than the structured and specialized system of *droit administratif* administered by the specialist public law courts in France, or the ability enjoyed by the United States judiciary to construe new legislation in light of defined constitutional rights.

The British judiciary, again as demonstrated in Chapter 4, may with ease choose not to interfere with what it views as 'political' decisions. In doing so, and in failing to observe or enforce the constitutional necessity of accountability for executive action, it leaves the constitutional arrangements vulnerable, and effectively misses an opportunity to embed rights of citizenship within the constitution.

Even when British courts do arrive at decisions that would appear to offer support for collective notions such as participation in decision-making processes, for example *Bradbury v Enfield* ([1967] 3 All ER 434), such decisions are neither derived from, nor allowed to develop into, principles that support broad constitutional ends. Rather, such cases are limited to their particular facts, based on the particular relevant statute, and may be readily avoided by future courts as British public law continues to develop in its *ad hoc*, unprincipled way.

This is not, however, an argument for the unelected judiciary to usurp the powers of an elected, majority government. Rather, it is an argument in favour of the development within British public law of devices, structures and principles, that ensure that executive action does not contravene broad democratic and constitutional aims. Thus, mechanisms must be devised which ensure that fundamental principles of constitutionality, such as equity, and rational discourse, are not allowed to wither at the hands of the executive; in effect, mechanisms that ensure that executive action moves towards fulfilling rather than undermining such constitutional goals.

It is possible that recent developments in the limited adoption and development of concepts such as proportionality and legitimate expectation may signal the development of a new, principle-oriented public law in Britain, though such moves remain the exception rather than the norm. Despite the very different constitutional positions, it seems likely that British public lawyers would be repaid by a study of devices such as hybrid rule-making and the hard look doctrine, both introduced as bolsters to the model of due process prevalent in the USA.

Such developments do not amount to the judiciary usurping legislative functions, as they represent procedural devices in the service of constitutionality, rather than establishing new substantive rights *per se*. It is of course true, as Longley (1993) demonstrates in relation to health care, that the application of such principles will have an impact upon decision-making processes, and hence may well influence outcomes such as distribution of resources; however, they remain devices requiring adherence to constitutional principles, rather than requiring any specific substantive outcome.

It would be difficult to deny, in light of the evidence considered in this book, that Britain stands in urgent need of such mechanisms, whether transplanted wholesale from abroad, or grafted onto existing structures. In the absence of such protection, not only will citizens, individually or collectively, find the public law system an untrustworthy ally in their efforts to enforce claims to substantive rights, but they will also find that the law fails to offer adequate protection for the political discourse within the constitutional arena in which they, as citizens, can legitimately expect to play a full part.

STEERING THE BOAT

The model of competition introduced into state education in Britain appears to have failed to attain any of its three targets. It has failed to offer any significant degree of empowerment to 'consumers'. It has failed to enhance the accountability of those who exercise power over schools. It has shown no evidence of leading to an improvement in educational standards.

The claim of recent reformers has been that power over education must be relocated from teaching professionals and the 'educational establishment', to a situation in which parents exercise ultimate control; a move from a position of producer domination to one of consumer sovereignty. However, the evidence suggests that somewhere in the course of this move, and whether by design or not, control of education has been captured by an elite, consisting of powerful headteachers and governors, middle-class parents, and bodies self-appointed from within such groups or appointed by central government. This new oligarchy, cutting across the divide 'between consumer and producer, has the potential to control the direction of the educational boat without being accountable to the other 'passengers'.

In the USA, experiments with the introduction of market forces into education have, in addition to enabling parents to exercise choice, actively sought to engage teachers, as service deliverers in the process of change (Osborne and Gaebler, 1992; and Sky 1992) in an effort to further 'ownership' of the education service by those most intimately connected with it, a move supported even by radical supporters of markets such as Coons (1986). In Britain, however, the tokenistic empowerment of parents has been accompanied by a significant reduction in the autonomy and influence of most teaching professionals, particularly in respect of curriculum requirements. The exception perhaps is those individual headteachers who now have a significant role to play in choosing the direction of our education system.

Rather than resulting in an increased sense of ownership of this public service by those involved with it, parents, teachers, and of course children, it has resulted in disillusionment and frustration by those who have had their expectations of choice falsely raised, or who feel increasingly unable to exercise their professional judgement. Indeed, it is not to go too far to suggest that far from increasing the kind of ownership discussed by Osborne and Gaebler, the British model has resulted in the potential for increased autocracy, symptomatic of the 'capture' of the service by relatively unaccountable power holders.

If we are to persist with a quasi-market in state education, and it seems unlikely that the present trend will be reversed in the foreseeable future, then new and appropriate structural devices must be created that act as checks on the exercise of power.

For effective citizenship, it is necessary to achieve a balance between representative and participative decision-making processes, ensuring that representatives are accountable, and that participation is meaningful. If the market is not to produce or reproduce autocracy and hierarchy, then it must be managed. In proposing new quangos, the government has already acknowledged the need for structural management, but the crucial issue for public lawyers is to address the issue of rendering accountable *whoever* is managing the market.

As Kirp (1976) notes, reliance on the introduction of new rights, whether substantive or procedural, must not be uncritically trusted as a cure for all the inequities existing in our educational arrangements. In practice, however, it seems that many of the current problems identified in this book could largely be addressed by procedural requirements embodying concepts of openness, provision of information adequate to allow informed participation, and the development of duties of reasoned decision making, all key elements observable in the somewhat stronger model of accountability existing in the USA.

The continuing existence of profound inequality in United States society demonstrates that such a system does indeed not provide all the answers to inequity in the distribution of society's resources, though equally, as Longley (1993) demonstrates in relation to the distribution of health care resources, such requirements can have a positive impact on the quality of decision making. A more profound realignment of the balance of privilege would require a more direct and wholesale effort at re-engineering society.

Few would argue that the previous model of LEA management was perfect. Though at its best local government can represent a sensitive and responsive mechanism for implementing the will of the local populace it has far too often fallen short of this ideal. The very limited involvement in local politics, typified by the low turn-outs at local government elections, demonstrates the failure to engage large sections of the population in the processes of political discourse, leaving the local government system itself open to capture by small, and potentially unrepresentative, politically active groups.

It can be argued that this demonstrates a need to increase participation in local government rather than to end local government, and that in practice LEAs were, and in so far as they continue to exercise limited functions, remain more accountable, via political and legal processes, than those who now hold power. This argument leads potentially to consideration of a system in which a locally elected and responsive local authority plays an interactive role with other agencies, local and national, seeking to facilitate choice, but also, with a primary function of ensuring that collective goals, such as equity, are served (Cordingley and Kogan, 1993).

It is possible that LEAs will emerge in this direction from the corner in which they presently find themselves, as the creation of local 'Schools Commissions', in Leeds (*Education*, 15 May 1992 and 3 June 1992) and Calderdale (Tonge, 1993) suggests. The Leeds Schools Commission, under an independent Chair, and made up of equal sized groups of headteachers, councillors and governors, plus, representatives of the local diocesan boards and race equality council has a brief to review the relationship of the LEA and local schools, maximizing delegation of powers to schools, but retaining an active role for the local authority. The move may well be informed primarily by the objective of deterring schools from opting-out, but nevertheless appears an interesting and positive development in the sharing of power and responsibility in the locality.

Osborne and Gaebler (1992) suggest, with reference to examples from a range of jurisdictions, that bureaucracy is not an adequate model of government in modern times, raising the question of with what should we replace it. To an extent, Osborne and Gaebler ignore the point made by Codd (1991), that reforms of the education system such as those seen in Britain, New Zealand and the USA, are contingent upon the acceptance of monetarist policies and the associated model of the state. The reforms fulfil the demands of the *Zeitgeist*, but are not necessarily indicative of the impossibility of designing bureaucratic administrative systems that effectively fulfil collective goals.

What we are faced with is not a simple choice between unconstrained market forces, and bureaucratic planning and control. The existing market based model retains a strong element of control and management. As this book has demonstrated, what has changed is the location of such powers, into the hands of relatively unaccountable individuals and bodies rather than democratically elected local authorities. On the other hand, any return to local bureaucratic planning would need to incorporate greatly enhanced mechanisms of informed participation, and choice, for citizens both individually and collectively.

The intention expressed by Osborne and Gaebler, and Lewis (1993b) to improve service standards by introducing, or mimicking, market situations and encouraging entrepreneurship within public services, is superficially attractive, though runs into certain difficulties in the British context. The threat is that such proposals do nothing to guarantee, and may substantially undermine, two vital aspects of citizenship. The empirical evidence relating to the outcomes of the recent reforms, discussed in Chapter 3, demonstrates how the existing arrangements, at the same time as failing to provide effective and widespread participation in community decision making, also produce highly inequitable outcomes in terms of service provision.

If the time has come, to borrow again Osborne and Gaebler's metaphor, for governments to stop 'rowing the boat', in the sense of providing public services, and instead to concentrate on 'steering', a number of possible alternative mechanisms exist.

The introduction of competition into areas such as education *may* provide a suitable means to achieving this goal, as may privatization of such services through the selling off of assets or the contracting-out of services, or the creation of hybrid public/private/non-profit ventures, or the development of new more-or-less autonomous agencies bound by framework agreements.

Osborne and Gaebler, and Lewis, acknowledge that no single one of these options provides the answer to reinventing government across the range of public services.

As Osborne and Gaebler demonstrate, these phenomena are being employed in a number of Western countries, and across a wide range of public services, nowhere more so than in Britain, where, despite Margaret Thatcher's stated aim of eliminating quangos, they flourished under her premiership, and indeed mutated into a new range of Next Steps agencies (Harden, 1987), and where in education, new public/private partnerships such as CTCs and Training and Enterprise Councils (TECs) already exist.

Though state education in Britain has not yet been privatized, in the sense of the selling-off of assets, the evidence presented in this book might well lead to the conclusion that a very real process of privatization has taken place, in the sense of schools having been removed from effective mechanisms of public accountability. The inherent risk in such a development is that, in the absence of effective mechanisms of public scrutiny, it will not be possible for citizens, or public lawyers, to ensure that constitutional and democratic expectations are fulfilled.

As Cordingley and Kogan (1993) note, each model of management represents a particular constellation of values, and it is crucial that those who believe in collective values resist the hegemonic power of individualism, embodied in recent reforms, and offer and develop alternative systems that better serve the needs of the wider community, and fulfil our expectations of equity.

Remembering the central importance of accountability to the legitimacy of government, the task which public lawyers, in Britain and elsewhere, have to address is the design of constitutional and legal structures that ensure effective and responsive steering, and that those in control of the tiller are effectively rendered accountable.

The direction taken by our school system is crucial, both for the well-being of the community as a whole and for our individual children. In a sense, it matters not who has control of the education system, provided that they have enough power and resources to perform the task, that they are responsive and accountable to the community, and ensure equitable distribution of the good – all fundamental expectations for a public education system.

Local authorities probably no longer have the power to fulfil such functions, and in any event themselves too often fell foul of the requirement of responsiveness before the ERA. However, if John Major is serious about his new citizenry, he should act on such concerns, and let government take the lead in devising systems that ensure that those managing the education system are accountable to the citizenry. If we fail in this task, as the evidence already strongly indicates, there is significant potential for the control over direction to be determined by powerful, self-appointed, and unaccountable 'new magistracies'. What then of citizenship? What then of political choice?

Cordingley and Kogan (1993) suggest that the failure of educational reforms to produce identifiable improvements in schooling, despite lavish expenditure on their introduction in times of financial stringency, is a matter that should come under the scrutiny of our political mechanisms of accountability. Perhaps the Public Accounts Committee would care to note this suggestion. However, in an era in which the executive dominates the national political processes, if our politicians are not able or willing to safeguard the citizen's interests in schooling, then it behoves the public lawyer, uniquely positioned as a guardian of expectations of equity and at the heart of the relationship between the state apparatus and citizens, to take on this task.

The implicit constitutional expectation of rationality in public decision making is manifestly ill-served by the existing system of public law. Not only does it fail to ensure timely, effective, wide-ranging and well-informed participation in decision making, but equally, the apparently perverse outcomes of cases decided under the concept of 'reasonableness', considered in Chapter 4, demonstrate that no effective channel exists for *ex post facto* challenge of executive decisions.

Though the education reforms discussed in this book demonstrate a radically different role for the British state in the 1990s when compared with the 1950s or 1960s, or even the 1980s, the need identified in Chapter 1, to develop an effective, principled, system of public law, adequate to ensure the constitutionality of action in the management of state schooling remains undiminished, whether it is managed directly by the state bureaucracy or by quasi-autonomous agencies or individuals.

It is equally unsatisfactory for an education system to fail our children, and for a system of public law to fail our constitutional expectations. This book has demonstrated the intimate connections between the constitution, administration, and the delivery of education. Reinventing the government of education as part of the current remodelling of the state provides the opportunity for, and indeed demands, a reassessment of our constitutional arrangements and the role played by the law. It seems an appropriate moment for us to reinvent public law.

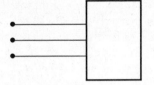

REFERENCES

Note: Publications by Ministry of Education, Department of Education and Science and Department for Education are all listed under DFE.

Adler, M. (1990) 'Rights as trumps: the case of parental choice in Scotland', *Education and the Law*, 2(2), 67.

Adler, M. (1993) 'Parental choice and the enhancement of children's interests', in P. Munn (ed.) *Parents and Schools: Customers, Managers or Partners*. London: Routledge.

Adler, M., Petch, A. and Tweedie, J. (1989) *Parental Choice and Educational Policy*. Edinburgh: Edinburgh University Press.

Ahier, J. and Flude, M. (eds) (1983) *Contemporary Education Policy*. London: Croom Helm.

Audit Commission (1989) *Losing an Empire, Finding a Role: The LEA of the Future*. London: HMSO.

Bash, L. and Coulby, D. (eds) (1989) *The Education Reform Act: Competition and Control*. London: Cassell.

Bastow, B. (1991) 'How to single out a school', *TES*, 2 August.

Beckett, F. (1991) 'Power to whom?', *Education*, 8 March.

Birkinshaw, P. (1985) *Grievances, Remedies and the State*. London: Sweet and Maxwell.

Birkinshaw, P., Harden, I. and Lewis, N. (1990) *Government by Moonlight: The Hybrid Parts of the State*. London: Unwin Hyman.

Bogdanor, V. (1991) 'Where will the buck stop?', *TES*, 14 June.

Briault, E. and Smith, F. (1980). *Falling Rolls in Secondary Schools*. Slough: NFER.

Brighouse, T. and Tomlinson, J. (1991) *Successful Schools*. London: Institute of Public Policy Research.

Brown, P. (1989) 'Education', in P. Brown and R. Sparks (eds) *Beyond Thatcherism*. Milton Keynes: Open University Press.

Bush, T. and Kogan, M. (1982) *Directors of Education*. London: George Allen and Unwin.

Bush, T., Kogan, M. and Lenney, T. (1989) *Directors of Education – Facing Reform*. London: Jessica Kingsley.

Cane, P. (1992) *An Introduction to Administrative Law*, 2nd edn. Oxford: Oxford University Press.

Chitty, C. (1989) *Towards a New Education System: The Victory of the New Right?* Lewes: Falmer.

Chitty, C. (1992) *The Education System Transformed*. Manchester: Baseline.

Codd, J. (1981) *Democratic principles and the politics of curriculum change in New Zealand'*, in M. Clark (ed.) *The Politics of Education in New Zealand*. Wellington: NZCER.

Codd, J. (1991) 'Curriculum reform in New Zealand', *Journal of Curriculum Studies*, 23(2).

Coons, J. (1986) 'Educational change and the courts: U.S. and Germany', *American Journal of Comparative Law*, 34(1), 1.

Coons, J. and Sugarman, S. (1978) *Education by Choice: The Case for Family Control*. Berkeley: University of California Press.

Cordingley, P. and Kogan, M. (1993) *In Support of Education*. London: Jessica Kingsley.

Dale, R. (1983) 'Thatcherism and education', in J. Ahier and M. Flude (eds) *Contemporary Education Policy*. London: Croom Helm.

Dale, R. (1989) *The State and Education Policy*. Milton Keynes: Open University Press.

Davies, B. and Anderson, L. (1992) *Opting for Self-Management*. London: Routledge.

DFE (1943) *Educational Reconstruction*. White Paper, Cmd 6458. London: HMSO.

DFE (1944) *Principles of Government*. White Paper, Cmd 6523. London: HMSO.

DFE (1959) *15–18: A Report of the Central Advisory Committee for Education* (Crowther Report). London: HMSO.

DFE (1963) *Half Our Future* (Newsom Report). London: HMSO.

DFE (1967) *Children and their Primary Schools* (Plowden Report). London: HMSO.

DFE (1977) *A New Partnership for Our Schools* (Taylor Report). London: HMSO.

DFE (1978) *The Composition of Governing Bodies*. White Paper, Cmnd 7430. London: HMSO.

DFE (1985) *Better Schools*. White Paper, Cmnd 9469. London: HMSO.

DFE (1987a) *Providing for Quality: The Pattern of Organisation to Age 19*. Circular 3/87. London: HMSO.

DFE (1987b) *Grant Maintained Schools: Consultation Paper*. London: HMSO.

DFE (1988) *Education Reform Act 1988: Grant-Maintained Schools*. Circular 10/88. London: HMSO.

DFE (1989a) *Grant Maintained Schools: Financial Arrangements*. Circular 21/89. London: HMSO.

DFE (1989b) *School Governors: How to Become a Grant-maintained School*, 2nd edn. London: HMSO.

DFE (1991) *The Parent's Charter: You and Your Child's Education*. London: HMSO.

DFE (1992) *Choice and Diversity: A New Framework for Schools*. White Paper, Cm 2021. London: HMSO.

de Smith, S. (1980) *Judicial Review of Administrative Action*, 4th edn. London: Stevens.

Echols, F., McPherson, A. and Willms, J. (1990) *Parental Choice in Scotland*. Edinburgh: Centre for Educational Sociology, University of Edinburgh.

Edwards, T., Gewirtz, S. and Whitty, G. (1992) 'Researching a policy in progress: the city technology colleges initiative', *Research Papers in Education*, 7(1), 79.

Edwards, T. and Whitty, G. (1992) 'Parental choice and educational reform in Britain and the United States', *British Journal of Educational Studies*, 40(2), 101.

Ehrlich, E. (1922) 'The sociology of law', *Harvard Law Review*, 36, 130.

Elliot, J. (1982) 'How do parents choose and judge secondary schools?', in R. McCormick, *Calling Education to Account*. Oxford: Heinemann/Open University.

Feintuck, M. (1993) The Impact of ERA 1988 on Accountability, Choice and Planning in the Schools' System, with Special Reference to GM Schools. University of Sheffield. Unpublished PhD thesis.

Fenwick, K. and MacBride, P. (1981) *The Government of Education in Britain*. Oxford: Martin Robertson.

Finch, J. (1984) *Education as Social Policy*. London: Longman.

Flude, M. and Hammer, M. (1990) *The Education Reform Act 1988: Its Origins and Its Implications*. Lewes: Falmer.

Galanter, M. (1975) 'Why the "haves" come out ahead: speculations on the limits of legal change', *Law and Society Review*, 9, 95.

Gamble, A. (1989) 'Privatisation, Thatcherism and the British state', *Journal of Law and Society*, 16(1), 1.

Gann, N. (1991) 'Left out in the cold', *TES* 4 January.

Garnett, M. (1993). 'Attractive, up to a point?', *Education*, 23 April.

Glennerster, H. (1991) 'Quasi-markets for education?', *Economic Journal*, 101, 1268.

Graham, C. and Prosser, T. (eds) (1988) *Waiving the Rules: The Constitution Under Thatcherism*. Milton Keynes: Open University Press.

Habermas, J. (1976) *Legitimation Crisis*. London: Heinemann.

Halpin, D., Power, S. and Fitz, J. (1991) 'Grant-maintained schools: making a difference without being really different', *British Journal of Educational Studies*, 39(4), 409.

Harden, I. (1987) 'A constitution for quangos', *Public Law*, 27.

Harden, I. (1990) 'The indirect public administration of education in Britain', in T. Modeen and A. Rosas (eds) *Indirect Public Administration in the Fields of Education and Pensions*. Åbo, Åbo: Academic Press.

Harden, I. and Lewis, N. (1986) *The Noble Lie: The British Constitution and the Rule of Law*. London: Hutchinson.

Haviland, J. (ed.) (1988) *Take Care Mr. Baker!* London: Fourth Estate.

Hill, M. (1976) *The State, Administration, and the Individual*. Glasgow: Fontana / Collins.

Hillgate Group (1986) *Whose Schools? A Radical Manifesto*. London: Hillgate Group.

Hinds, W. (1991) 'Judicial review and education: an overview', *Education and the Law*, 3(3), 139.

Hirschman, A. (1970) *Exit, Voice and Loyalty: Responses to Declines in Firms, Organizations and States*. Cambridge, MA.: Harvard University Press.

Hodges, L. (1991) 'Nightmare scenario?', *Education*, 1 March.

Howell, D. (1981) 'Problems of school government', in B. Simon and W. Taylor (eds) *Education in the Eighties*. London: Batsford.

Humes, W. (1986) *The Leadership Class in Scottish Education*. Edinburgh: John Donald.

ILEA (Inner London Education Authority) (1976) *William Tyndale Junior and Infants Schools Public Inquiry: A Report to the ILEA* (Auld Report). London: ILEA.

Johnson, D. (1990) *Parental Choice in Education*. London: Unwin Hyman.

Jonathan, R. (1993) 'Parental rights in schooling', in P. Munn (ed.) *Parents and Schools: Customers, Managers or Partners*. London: Routledge.

Jones, C. (1989) 'The break-up of the ILEA', in L. Bash and D. Coulby (eds) *The Education Reform Act: Competition and Control*. London: Cassell.

Jung, D. and Kirp, D. (1984) 'Law as an instrument of educational policy-making', *American Journal of Comparative Law*, 32(4), 625.

Kahn-Freund, O. (1974) 'On uses and misuses of comparative law', *Modern Law Review*, 37(1), 1.

Kellas, J. (1984) *The Scottish Political System*, 3rd edn. Cambridge: Cambridge University Press.

Kent County Council (1978) *Education Vouchers in Kent: A Feasibility Study*. Canterbury: KCC.

Kirp, D. (1976) 'Proceduralism and bureaucracy: due process in the school setting', *Stanford Law Review*, 28 (May), 841.

Knight, C. (1990) *The Making of Tory Education Policy in Post-War Britain, 1950–1986*. Lewes: Falmer.

Kogan, M. and van der Eyken, W. (1973) *County Hall*. Harmondsworth: Penguin.

Kogan, M. (1978) *The Politics of Educational Change*. London: Fontana.

Kogan, M. (1988) *Education Accountability: An Analytic Overview*, 2nd edn. London: Hutchinson.

Lawlor, S. (1988a) *Opting-Out – A Guide to Why and How*. London: Centre for Policy Studies.

Lawlor, S. (1988b) *Away With LEAs – ILEA Abolition as a Pilot*. London: Centre for Policy Studies.

Lawson, J. and Silver, H. (1973) *A Social History of Education in England*. London: Methuen.

Lawton, D. (ed.) (1989) *The Education Reform Act: Choice and Control*. London: Hodder and Stoughton.

Le Grand, J. (1989) 'Markets, welfare and equality', in J. Le Grand and S. Estrin (eds) *Market Socialism*. Oxford: Clarendon.

Le Grand, J. (1991) 'Quasi-markets and social policy', *Economic Journal*, 101, 1256.

Lewis, N. and Birkinshaw, P. (1979) 'Taking complaints seriously: a study in local government practice', in M. Partington and J. Jowell (eds). *Welfare Law and Policy*. London: Frances Pinter.

Lewis, N. (1993a) 'Markets, regulation and citizenship: a constitutional analysis', in R. Brownsword (ed.) *Law and the Public Interest*. Stuttgart: Franz Steiner.

Lewis, N. (1993b) *How to Reinvent British Government*. London: European Policy Forum.

Lewis, N., Seneviratne, M. and Cracknell, S. (1987) *Complaints Procedures in Local Government*. Sheffield: Centre for Criminological and Socio-Legal Research, University of Sheffield.

Lister, E. (1991) *LEAs – Old and New*. London: Centre for Policy Studies.

Local Schools Information (1992) *Opting-Out 1988–1992: An Analysis*. London: LSI.

Longley, D. (1990) 'Diagnostic dilemmas: accountability in the NHS', *Public Law*, 527.

Longley, D. (1993) *Public Law and Health Service Accountability*. Buckingham: Open University Press.

Loughlin, M. (1989) 'Law, ideologies and the political-administrative system', *Journal of Law and Society*, 16(1), 21.

Maclure, S. (1988) *Education Re-Formed*. London: Hodder and Stoughton. (See also 3rd edn, 1992).

McPherson, A. and Raab, C. (1988) *Governing Education – a Sociology of Policy Since 1945*. Edinburgh: Edinburgh University Press.

Maynard, A. (1975) *Experiment with Choice in Education*. London: Institute of Economic Affairs.

Meredith, P. (1985) 'Case note: R v South Glamorgan Appeals Committee *ex parte* Evans, Div. Ct. CO/197/84', *Journal of Social Welfare Law*, May, 162.

Meredith, P. (1992) *Government, Schools and the Law*. London: Routledge.

Miliband, D. (1991) *Markets, Politics and Education*. London: Institute of Public Policy Research.

Milman, D. (1986) *Educational Conflict and the Law*. London: Routledge and Kegan Paul.

Mitchell, J.D.B. (1965) 'The causes and effects of the absence of a system of public law in the United Kingdom', *Public Law*, 95.

Moore, D. (1990) 'Voice and choice in Chicago', in W. Clune and J. Witte (eds) *Choice and Control in American Education, Vol. 2*. London and New York: Falmer.

Moran, M. (1988) 'Politics and law in financial regulation', in C. Graham and T. Prosser (eds) *Waiving the Rules: The Constitution under Thatcherism*. Milton Keynes: Open University Press.

Mortimore, P. (1992) 'Quality control in education and schools', *British Journal of Educational Studies*, 40(1), 23.

Munn, P. (1991) 'School boards, accountability and control', *British Journal of Educational Studies*, 39(2), 173.

Munn, P. (ed.) (1993) *Parents and Schools: Customers, Managers or Partners*. London: Routledge.

National Commission on Education (1993) *An Alternative Approach to Parental Choice*. NCE Briefing No. 13. London: NCE.

National Consumer Council (1992) *When Things Go Wrong at School?* London: NCC.

Ofsted (1993) *Grant Maintained Schools 1988–92*. London: HMSO.

Osborne, D. and Gaebler, T. (1992) *Reinventing Government*. New York: Addison-Wesley.

Page, A. (1987) 'Financial services: the self-regulatory alternative', in R. Baldwin and C. McCrudden, *Regulation and Public Law*. London: Weidenfeld and Nicolson.

Parker, A. (1993) 'Charter schools in the USA', *Education*, 26 March and 2 April.

Parker-Jenkins, M. (1992) 'Beware the British solution', *Education*, 31 January.

Partington, J. and Wragg, T. (1989) *Schools and Parents*. London: Cassell.

Petch, A. (1986) 'Parents' reasons for choosing secondary schools', in A. Stillman (ed.) *The Balancing Act of 1980: Parents, Politics and Education*. Slough: NFER.

Prosser, T. (1982) 'Towards a critical public law', *Journal of Law and Society*, 9(1), 1.

Raab, C. (1993) 'Parents and schools: what role for education authorities?', in P. Munn (ed.) *Parents and Schools: Customers, Managers or Partners*. London: Routledge.

Ranson, S. (1988) 'From 1944 to 1988; education, citizenship and democracy', *Local Government Studies*, 14(1), 1.

Ranson, S. (1990a) *The Politics of Reorganizing Schools*. London: Unwin Hyman.

Ranson, S. (1990b) From 1944 to 1988: education, citizenship and democracy', in M. Flude and M. Hammer, *The Education Reform Act 1988: Its Origins and Its Implications*. Lewes: Falmer.

Ranson, S. and Stewart, J. (1989) 'Citizenship and government: the challenge for management in the public domain', *Political Studies*, 37, 5.

Riddell, S. and Brown, S. (eds) (1991) *School Effectiveness Research*. Edinburgh: HMSO.

Riley, K.A. (1992) 'The changing framework and purposes of education authorities', *Research Papers in Education*, 7(1).

Rogers, M. (1992) *Opting Out: Choice and the Future of Schools*. London: Lawrence and Wishart.

Ross, A. and Tomlinson, S. (1991) *Teachers and Parents: New Roles, New Relationships*. London: Institute of Public Policy Research.

Sallis, J. (1988) *Schools, Parents and Governors: A New Approach to Accountability*. London: Routledge.

Salter, B. and Tapper, T. (1981) *Education, Politics and the State*. London: Grant McIntyre.

Sams, B. (1991) 'New chartism, no choice', *Education*, 8 November.

Schwartz, B. and Wade, H.W.R. (1972) *Legal Control of Government*. Oxford: Clarendon.

SOED (Scottish Office Education Department) (1993) *Guidelines on the Structure and Balance of the Curriculum*. Circular 5/93. Edinburgh: HMSO.

Seldon, A. (1986) *The Riddle of the Voucher*. London: Institute of Economic Affairs.

Sharp, P. and Dunford, J. (1990) *The Education System in England and Wales*. Harlow: Longman.

Simon, B. (1988) *Bending the Rules – the Baker 'Reform' of Education.* London: Lawrence and Wishart.

Simon, B. (1992) *What Future for Education?* London: Lawrence and Wishart.

Simon, B. and Taylor, W. (eds) (1981) *Education in the Eighties.* London: Batsford.

Sky, T. (1989) 'Law and the system of elementary and secondary education in the United States', *Education and the Law*, 1(2), 69.

Sky, T. (1992) 'Open enrollment legislation in the United States and the United Kingdom: some comparative notes', *Education and the Law*, 4(2), 75.

Stewart, R.B. (1975) 'The reformation of American administrative law', *Harvard Law Review*, 88(8), 1669.

Stillman, A. (ed.) (1986) *The Balancing Act of 1980: Parents, Politics and Education.* Slough: NFER.

Stillman, A. (1990) 'Legislating for choice', in M. Flude and M. Hammer, *The Education Reform Act 1988: Its Origins and Its Implications.* Lewes: Falmer.

Templeton, J. (1989) 'Creation of a home school council in a secondary school', in S. Wolfendale (ed.) *Parental Involvement.* London: Cassell.

Tonge, J. (1993) 'A new role for LEAs without leaving some schools unsupported?', *Education*, 23 April.

Walford, G. (1990) 'Developing choice in British education', *Compare*, 20(1).

Walford, G. (1991) 'Choice of school at the first city technology college', *Educational Studies*, 17(1), 65.

Warnock, M. (1988) *A Common Policy for Education.* Oxford: Oxford University Press.

Welsh Office (1988a) *Educational Quality in Wales: The Response to Falling Schools' Rolls.* Circular 20/88. Cardiff: HMSO.

Welsh Office (1988b) *Education Reform Act 1988: Grant Maintained Schools.* Circular 49/88. Cardiff: HMSO.

West, A. and Varlaam A. (1991) 'Choice of high schools: pupils' perceptions', *Educational Research*, 33(3), 205.

Whitty, G. and Menter, I. (1989) 'Lessons of Thatcherism: education policy in England and Wales 1979–1988', *Journal of Law and Society*, 16(1), 42.

Whitty, G., Fitz, J. and Edwards, T. (1989) 'Assisting whom? Benefits and costs of the assisted places scheme', in A. Hargreaves and D. Reynolds (eds) *Education Policies: Controversies and Critiques.* Falmer, New York.

Wragg, T. (1988) *Education in the Market Place.* London: NUT.

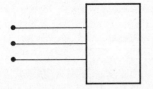

INDEX